THE DAILY STUDY BIBLE

(OLD TESTAMENT)

General Editor: John C. L. Gibson

JEREMIAH

Vol. 2

JEREMIAH

Volume 1

ROBERT DAVIDSON

THE WESTMINSTER PRESS
PHILADELPHIA

Scripture quotations from the Revised Standard Version of the Bible are copyrighted 1946, 1952, © 1971, 1973 by the Division of Christian Education of the National Council of the Churches of Christ in the U.S.A., and are used by permission of the National Council of Churches, New York, and William Collins Sons & Co., Ltd., Glasgow.

Published by
The Saint Andrew Press
Edinburgh, Scotland
and
The Westminster Press ®
Philadelphia, Pennsylvania

Printed in the United States of America

Library of Congress Cataloging in Publication Data

Davidson, Robert.
    Jeremiah.

    (The Daily study Bible series)
    Bibliography: v. 1, p.
    1. Bible. O.T. Jeremiah—Commentaries. I. Title.
II. Series: Daily study Bible series (Westminster Press)
BS1525.3.D38 1983   224'.207'7   83-14598

ISBN 0-664-21394-4 (v. 1)
ISBN 0-664-24476-9 (pbk. : v. 1)

GENERAL PREFACE

The series of commentaries on the Old Testament, to which this first volume on *Jeremiah* by Professor Davidson belongs, has been planned as a companion series to the much-acclaimed New Testament series of the late Professor William Barclay. As with that series, each volume is arranged in successive headed portions suitable for daily study. The Biblical text followed is that of the Revised Standard Version or Common Bible. Eleven contributors share the work, each being responsible for from one to three volumes. The series is issued in the hope that it will do for the Old Testament what Professor Barclay's series succeeded so splendidly in doing for the New Testament—make it come alive for the Christian believer in the twentieth century.

Its two-fold aim is the same as his. Firstly, it is intended to introduce the reader to some of the more important results and fascinating insights of modern Old Testament scholarship. Most of the contributors are already established experts in the field with many publications to their credit. Some are younger scholars who have yet to make their names but who in my judgment as General Editor are now ready to be tested. I can assure those who use these commentaries that they are in the hands of competent teachers who know what is of real consequence in their subject and are able to present it in a form that will appeal to the general public.

The primary purpose of the series, however, is *not* an academic one. Professor Barclay summed it up for his New Testament series in the words of Richard of Chichester's prayer—to enable men and women "to know Jesus Christ more clearly, to love Him more dearly, and to follow Him more nearly." In the case of the Old Testament we have to be a little more circumspect than that. The Old Testament was completed long before the time of Our Lord, and it was (as it still is) the sole Bible of the Jews, God's first people, before it became part of the Christian Bible. We must take this fact seriously.

Yet in its strangely compelling way, sometimes dimly and sometimes directly, sometimes charmingly and sometimes embarrassingly, it holds up before us the things of Christ. It should not be forgotten that Jesus Himself was raised on this Book, that He based His whole ministry on what it says, and that He approached His death with its words on His lips. Christian men and women have in this ancient collection of Jewish writings a uniquely illuminating avenue not only into the will and purposes of God the Father, but into the mind and heart of Him who is named God's Son, who was Himself born a Jew but went on through the Cross and Resurrection to become the Saviour of the world. Read reverently and imaginatively the Old Testament can become a living and relevant force in their everyday lives.

It is the prayer of myself and my colleagues that this series may be used by its readers and blessed by God to that end.

New College   JOHN C. L. GIBSON
Edinburgh   General Editor

CONTENTS

Introduction 1

A. THE MAKING OF A PROPHET (CH.1)

The man (1:1–3)... 7
The age of crisis (1:1–3) (cont'd) 8
How it began: The call (1:4–10).......................... 10
How it began: The response and the reassurance (1:4–10)
(cont'd) 12
Two visions (i) (1:11–19) 15
Two visions (ii) (1:11–19) (cont'd) 17

B. GOD'S PEOPLE—IN THE WRONG AND ON THE WAY TO DISASTER (CHS. 2–6)

God's people in the wrong (2:1–6:30).................... 19
God's people on the way to disaster (2:1–6:30) (cont'd) 21
A strange case of infidelity (i) (2:1–13) 23
A strange case of infidelity (ii) (2:1–13) (cont'd) 26
The innocent and the guilty (2:14–19).................... 28
A people's tragedy and desperate plight (2:20–28) 30
Face the facts (2:29–37)................................. 33
Is reconciliation possible? (3:1–5) 35
Some people never learn (3:6–11) 37
The call to reconciliation (3:12–18) 39
The essentials for true reconciliation (3:19–4:4) 42
Coming disaster and the reasons for it (4:5–10)............. 44
Sound the alarm (4:5–10) (cont'd)........................ 46
The searing wind of judgement (4:11–18)...... 49
The prophet's agony (4:19–28)................ 50
A community without excuse (4:29–5:9) 53
A faithless community under judgement (i) (5:10–31) 56
A faithless community under judgement (ii) (5:10–31) (cont'd) 58
Jerusalem under siege—A final warning (6:1–8) 61
For whom the bell tolls (6:9–15) 62
Wrong choices (6:16–21)................................. 65

The role of the prophet (6:22–30) 68

C. FALSE RELIGION (7:1–8:3)

An unpopular sermon (i) *(7:1–15)* 69
An unpopular sermon (ii) *(7:1–15)* *(cont'd)* 72
The time for prayer is over (7:16–20) 74
A people blind to essentials (7:21–28) 76
A fatal disease (7:29–8:3) 77

D. THE END OF THE ROAD (8:4–10:25)

Blind complacency (8:4–12) 79
A people in despair: A prophet in anguish (8:13–9:1) 82
The prophet in despair (9:2–11) 85
A time for mourning (9:12–22) 88
Intermission (i) *(9:23–10:16)* 90
Intermission (ii) *(9:23–10:16)* *(cont'd)* 93
Tragedy and response (10:17–25) 95

E. THE MAN OF ACTION ... AND INNER CONFLICTS (CHS. 11–20)

The broken covenant and its dire consequences (11:1–17) 99
The cost of being a prophet (11:18–12:6) 102
The Lord of all nations (12:7–17) 107
The spoiled linen waistcloth (13:1–14) 110
Final words of warning (13:15–27) 113
A national crisis (14:1–16) 116
A further lament and comment (14:17–15:4) 121
Jerusalem left to her fate (15:5–9) 124
Inner struggles (i) *(15:10–21)* 125
Inner struggles (ii) *(15:10–21)* *(cont'd)* 128
Normal life at an end (16:1–13) 131
Light in the midst of darkness (16:14–21) 134
The indelible mark of sin (17:1–4) 137
The choice—Trust in man or trust in God (17:5–8) 139
Folly and hope (17:9–13) 141
A cry for help (17:14–18) 143
A sermon on sabbath observance (17:19–27) 145
In the potter's workshop (18:1–12) 148
Strangely unnatural conduct (18:13–17) 150
Opposition and a vitriolic response (18:18–23) 152

CONTENTS

The broken jar... (19:1–13)............................ 155
...And its consequences (19:14–20:6) 157
Insidious doubt and confident faith (20:7–13) 159
The depths of despair (20:14–18)....................... 163

Further Reading.. 166

INTRODUCTION

It is not easy to read through or to understand one of the lengthy prophetic books in the Old Testament. "The book of Jeremiah" naturally suggests to us a book written by a man called Jeremiah. Yet anyone who sits down and seriously tries to read through this book from beginning to end must soon begin to doubt this. If this book was written by a sane man with an orderly mind, he has done his best to confuse us. It is scrappy, built up of many bits and pieces which do not always seem to follow on easily from one another. It is badly ordered. Chapter 21, for example, tells of an incident in the reign of the last king of Judah, Zedekiah, but chapter 26 describes a sermon preached by Jeremiah at the beginning of the reign of one of his predecessors some twenty years earlier. The first verse of the book begins with "the words of Jeremiah". Since the Hebrew *davar*, "word", can refer to something spoken, a word, or something done, a deed or event, this phrase could be translated "the story, or the biography, of Jeremiah". But it is an odd biography; and we are left with a biographer with an exceedingly untidy mind. He would have had his manuscript returned with a rejection slip from any modern publisher.

To understand the book we have got to remember one thing. Most of the Old Testament prophets were not primarily writers; they were *preachers* who spoke rather than wrote the word that God gave them. One of the best illustrations of this, curiously enough, is to be found in chapter 36 which speaks of a book or a scroll. It is the year 604 B.C. The prophet dictates a scroll to his secretary Baruch, a scroll that was to contain all the words that Jeremiah had spoken in obedience to God up to that moment.

Two things are interesting about this scroll:

(1) If, as seems likely, Jeremiah began his ministry as a prophet in the year 627 B.C., he had already been a prophet for over twenty years before he felt the need to put down in writing what he had been saying to his people. During these years he had been preaching and teaching, as many other prophets did, and as Jesus did, by word of mouth. We must never forget that behind the written word in most prophetic books there lies the spoken word. We can feel this spoken word reaching out for us through the written word. It is characteristic of such preaching that again and again it comes back to the same themes and indeed uses the same illustrations, often in different sermons. Witness any popular preacher or evangelist today. Moreover, how we interpret the written word often depends on how we think the words were spoken, the tone of voice, the implied question, the hint of sarcasm. A good illustration of this is the different translations of 6:14 where Jeremiah is attacking prophets and priests for saying, according to the RSV:

> ... 'Peace, peace,'
> when there is no peace.

But the NEB translates:

> ... 'All is well.'
> All well? Nothing is well!

"Peace" and "All is well" are both reasonable translations of the Hebrew word *shalom*, but notice how when we come to the second *shalom* the NEB, perhaps rightly, implies a change of voice, a question.

(2) But why did Jeremiah feel the need to put his teaching into writing at this particular time? Probably because, as a result of his highly unpopular Temple Sermon (see chapters 7 and 26), he was *persona non grata* to the religious and political establishment. There were threats to his life; he was debarred from preaching in person in the Temple precincts. In this situation, and perhaps increasingly convinced of the urgency of his message of judge-

ment, he dictates the scroll to Baruch. Baruch can read it to the people: the word must continue to be heard, even if the prophet himself is banned from speaking it. When the king confiscates the scroll, slashes it with a knife and consigns the pieces to the fire, Jeremiah redictates his words to Baruch for inclusion in another scroll and adds a few further comments for good measure.

ITS VARIED CONTENTS

If the scroll of chapter 36 is the original spring out of which our present book of Jeremiah flows, many other rivulets have made their contribution before the book reaches us in its present form. Let us look briefly at some of the richly varied material in the book.

(1) There are passages which are concerned mainly with the word that came to the prophet from God. They are usually fairly brief passages, poetic in form. We call them prophetic oracles. They are introduced by a phrase such as "Thus says the Lord" (6:6, 9, 16, 22) or "Hear the word of the Lord" (2:4; 10:1). Sometimes they end with a phrase which the RSV translates "says the Lord". Turn to the beginning of chapter 2 and you will find a very good example of such a brief prophetic oracle in 2:2–3:

> Thus says the Lord,
> > I remember the devotion of your youth,
> > > your love as a bride,
> > how you followed me in the wilderness,
> > > in a land not sown.
> > Israel was holy to the Lord,
> > > the first fruits of his harvest.
> > All who ate of it became guilty;
> > > evil came upon them,
> > > > > says the Lord.

Notice the way in which Hebrew poetry achieves its effect by the use of balancing or parallel phrases. In verse 2, "the devotion of your youth" echoed by "your love as a bride"; "in the wilderness" echoed by "in a land not sown". In such oracles the prophet stands before us as God's messenger to the people of God. In the ancient world if you wanted to send a message to someone you could not pop it into an envelope and take it to the nearest pillar-box. You sent a personal messenger, who memorised the message you wished to deliver and then went and spoke it in your name and in your words, introducing the words by "Thus says my master". You will find a good example of this in Gen. 32:3–5. The prophet is just such a messenger, God's messenger.

(2) In addition to these brief poetic oracles there are longer prose passages, often in the form of sermons in a style and language very similar to that found in the book of Deuteronomy, e.g. 7:1–8:3; 11:1–17. There has been much discussion among scholars as to whether these sermons in their present form come from Jeremiah himself or whether they are the work of later preachers, taking Jeremiah's ideas and adapting them to make them relevant to the changed situation of their own day when most of the Jewish people were in exile in Babylon. It hardly detracts from the value of these sermons if, in their present form, they do not come from Jeremiah: indeed it but serves to underline the vitality of his message. Far from being only for his own age, it was capable of being reshaped to speak to other situations—and it has done so ever since.

(3) The book of Jeremiah contains an unusual amount of bio-graphical information, beginning with the account of a dramatic sermon which the prophet preached in Jerusalem in the autumn of 609 or the winter of 609/608 B.C. (see chapters 7 and 26) and continuing down to and including the fall of Jerusalem to the Babylonians in 587 B.C. In the last glimpse we have of him, we find him among Jewish exiles from that catastrophe in Egypt (chapter 44). In no sense is this information a complete biography. Rather it is a series of memoirs, mainly concerned with situations of conflict in which the prophet was involved. Some of these memoirs may come from the pen of Jeremiah's friend and sec-retary Baruch. Much of this material is to be found in chapters 26–45 of the present book.

(4) At various points in the book there are intensely personal autobiographical passages which, when taken together, make up

what has been called Jeremiah's "Confessions" or "Personal Spiritual Diary". Such passages—they include 11:18–12:6; 15:10–21; 17:5–10, 14–18; 18:18–23; 20:7–18—have no parallel in other prophetic books in the Old Testament. They seem to be modelled on—they may indeed have influenced—some of the Psalms, e.g. Psalm 73. For a few brief moments in these passages the veil which conceals from us the inner life of a prophet is lifted. We not only hear Jeremiah publicly preaching, we listen to him wrestling, agonising in prayer. Not only may we admire the courage he displayed in the face of opposition, but we glimpse something of the uncertainties, the black moods of despair and bitterness which lie behind such courage. Above all we see a man baring his soul to God, locked in conflict with God, a man for whom the way of faith was not easy, a man who could accuse God of deceiving him. This is a very human prophet, touched with our weaknesses, haunted by the kind of doubts which plague us.

All this is but a sample of the rich tapestry which is the book of Jeremiah. Many hands have woven its strands. We can see within the book certain clear patterns as deliberate attempts have been made to gather together material on related topics. Thus 23:9–40 is headed "Concerning the prophets", while chapters 27–29 recount incidents involving Jeremiah in conflict with other prophets. Chapters 30–33, often called "the book of consolation", gather together a series of passages whose dominant theme is hope for the future; while chapters 46–51 contain a collection of oracles against other nations. The book ends in chapter 52 with an extract from 2 Kings chapters 24–25.

ITS TWO FORMS

Not only is this not a book written by one man, Jeremiah, but it has come down to us across the centuries in two forms. The one, which we now read in our English versions including the RSV, goes back to what became the standard Hebrew text by the beginning of the Christian era. The other is found in the Greek version of the Old Testament, the Bible of the early church, and behind it there lies a different Hebrew text. It is considerably shorter and the material in it is, at certain points, differently ordered. The collection of the oracles against other nations, for example, which in the RSV appears in chapters 46–51, comes in the Greek text after 25:13 following the words "everything written in this book, which Jeremiah prophesied against all the nations", and the separate oracles within this collection come in a different order. It is impossible to say which form of the text takes us closest to the original book of Jeremiah, if there ever was one such book.

A GREAT PROPHET

There are thus many problems about the book of Jeremiah and its composition. But it is not our task in this commentary to concern ourselves too much with academic matters. However the book got its present shape, we can be sure of one thing. Through all its pages there come to us the message and activities of a great prophet, courageous and vulnerable, sensitive and passionate, a man almost crucified by his contemporaries, but canonised by later generations. There is much to shame us here, much to inspire us, and much from which we can learn.

A. THE MAKING OF A PROPHET (CH. 1)

There seem to be two basic ingredients in the making of a prophet in the Old Testament:

(1) a situation of crisis in which the community has lost, or is in danger of losing, its way. Often it is a crisis whose meaning and challenge are not recognised either by the religious establishment or by the man in the street.

(2) a personal experience in which a man finds himself gripped by God and commissioned to proclaim to the community a message which speaks to this crisis situation.

THE MAN

Jeremiah 1:1–3

> ¹The words of Jeremiah, the son of Hilkiah, of the priests who were in Anathoth in the land of Benjamin, ²to whom the word of the Lord came in the days of Josiah the son of Amon, king of Judah, in the thirteenth year of his reign. ³It came also in the days of Jehoiakim the son of Josiah, king of Judah, and until the end of the eleventh year of Zedekiah, the son of Josiah, king of Judah, until the captivity of Jerusalem in the fifth month.

Like many other prophetic books (e.g. Amos, Isaiah) this book begins with a brief introduction providing us with basic information about the prophet and the age in which he lived.

We are told something about Jeremiah's family background. He was born into a priestly family, "the son of Hilkiah, of the priests who were in Anathoth in the land of Benjamin". We may be sure that this profoundly influenced his life. He would be brought up to be familiar with the religious traditions of his people, the story of God's gracious dealings with Israel, the teaching about the kind of obedience for which God looked in return. For the priests were the parish ministers of ancient Israel, exercising an all-important teaching ministry in the community. If, at a later date, Jeremiah has some sharply critical things to say about the priests (e.g. 2:8; 8:8–12) it is not that he is rebelling against his upbringing or that he is by temperament anti-priestly. His charge is always that the priests are failing to fulfil their high calling to instruct the people in the ways of God.

His home was in Anathoth, a small village of no great importance a few miles north-east of Jerusalem; near enough for him to know what was going on in the big city, far enough away to make him a country lad who uses the familiar sights and sounds of the countryside to illustrate his message. Anathoth makes a brief appearance earlier in the Old Testament story. One of King David's staunchest supporters among the priests in Jerusalem was a man called Abiathar. On David's death Abiathar had the misfortune to back the wrong horse in the succession stakes. When Solomon came to power Abiathar was banished from court circles in Jerusalem to Anathoth. It may be that Jeremiah's family traced its ancestry back to Abiathar. Jeremiah was thus the son of a country manse, born into a family which had deep roots in the ministry. If this suggests a somewhat sheltered early life, becoming a prophet soon altered that. What kind of a man he became as he faced up to the challenge of being a prophet will become clearer as we study the book.

THE AGE OF CRISIS

Jeremiah 1:1–3 (*cont'd*)

We do not know when Jeremiah was born, but if the information given in verse 2 is correct he began his prophetic ministry in the year 627 B.C., the thirteenth year of the reign of King Josiah. His ministry then spanned the next forty turbulent years which witnessed the death throes of his people. The information given in these opening verses is not complete. Although it lists the major kings who occupied the throne of Judah in the last fifty years of its existence as an independent state, Josiah (640–609), Jehoiakim (609–598) and Zedekiah (597–587), it has nothing to say about the brief three-month rule of Josiah's son Jehoahaz or the equally brief reign of Jehoiakim's successor Jehoiachin, both of whom were deposed to make way for regimes which would be more acceptable to the imperial overlord of the day (2 Kings 23:31ff.; 2 Kings 24:8ff.).

When Jeremiah began his ministry there were signs of hope. Dark clouds seemed to be lifting. For much of the seventh century B.C. King Manasseh had kept Judah at peace by assiduously licking the boots of his Assyrian masters. But it was peace at a price; the price of accepting into Jerusalem the worship of Assyrian and other gods, of opening the flood-gates to dark superstitions like human sacrifice, the price of crushing the voices of protest. Now Manasseh and his short-lived son and successor (Amon) were dead. The power of the Assyrian empire was on the wane. Under King Josiah there was talk of religious reformation and national independence, talk which was to bear fruit in a solemn act of national reformation and renewal in the year 621 B.C. During repairs to the precincts of the Jerusalem Temple a book had been discovered, probably part of our present book of Deuteronomy, and this book provided the reforming party with its manifesto (see 2 Kings chs. 22–23).

The reformation had wide popular and official backing. It appealed to long thwarted nationalistic and religious instincts. What Jeremiah's attitude to it was we cannot be certain. He may have initially supported it: if so, he was soon to be disillusioned. You can legislate for reform, you can call a nation to an act of national repentance only to find that, after the emotional excitement of the mass rallies has passed, you are left with an enlightened statute book and a people basically unchanged. Certainly after the death of Josiah in 609 B.C. Jeremiah found himself increasingly alienated from the resurgent nationalism of the day; that it was a religious nationalism only made it the more dangerous. He protested against political and religious policies which he proved powerless to change and which signed the death-warrant of his people. Accused of being a traitor to his country and his country's religion, he bore a costly witness to unpalatable truths in the midst of national tragedy which culminated in the destruction of Jerusalem by the Babylonians in 587 B.C. By doing so he was able to act as midwife at the birth of a faith which enabled his people to see in their own tragedy the working out of the purposes of their God. When other nations perished, their gods tended to disappear; when Judah perished, new faith rose phoenix-like from the ashes of Jerusalem. If this was the Lord's doing, his agent was Jeremiah.

HOW IT BEGAN: THE CALL

Jeremiah 1:4–10

4Now the word of the Lord came to me saying,
5"Before I formed you in the womb I knew you,
and before you were born I consecrated you;
I appointed you a prophet to the nations."
6Then I said, "Ah, Lord God! Behold, I do not know how to speak,
for I am only a youth." 7But the Lord said to me,
"Do not say, 'I am only a youth';
for to all to whom I send you you shall go,
and whatever I command you you shall speak.
8Be not afraid of them,
for I am with you to deliver you, says the Lord."
9Then the Lord put forth his hand and touched my mouth; and the Lord said to me,
"Behold, I have put my words in your mouth.
10See, I have set you this day over nations and over kingdoms,
to pluck up and to break down,
to destroy and to overthrow,
to build and to plant."

Neither family background or influence, nor a situation of crisis in themselves, however, make a man a prophet. The Old Testament prophets come from all walks of life, from different social classes, from town and country. They have only this in common: they believe that God has stepped into their lives and called them into his service. This is their point of no return, an encounter with

God. Old Testament prophets describe this encounter in many different ways, presumably because it came to them in many different ways. There is no one, and only one, valid type of religious experience, as some people seem to claim. Amos says simply, "The Lord took me from following the flock and said 'Go...'" (Amos 7:15). Isaiah describes a vision which came to him in the Temple at Jerusalem (Isa. ch. 6). Here is Jeremiah's encounter.

"Now the word of the Lord came to me saying..." We are not told how it came, but in this encounter we can see certain elements which are almost always present when a man becomes a prophet in the Old Testament.

(1) There is first of all *a sense of God's call*. God interferes, he intrudes uninvited into a man's life. Yet at this very moment when God interferes, life takes on a new meaning. Jeremiah discovers who he is and what the true purpose of his life is, at the moment when he is arrested by God. This is it; the luminous moment for which unknowingly he had been waiting:

Before I formed you in the womb I knew you. (verse 5)

All along God had *known* him and this "know" is a word that often points to a deeply personal experience or relationship, such as that of husband and wife (Gen. 4:1) or God and his people. This relationship means that God has chosen him, for this knowing has a purpose. "I consecrated you...", literally "I made you holy" or I set you apart. The Hebrew word *qadosh*, holy, which lies behind the verb used here, is a word that points to God's own nature, to that which makes him different from us; and it also describes anything or anyone who is particularly associated with God or set apart for his service.

This service to which Jeremiah is called is described as that of being "a prophet to the nations". He is called to be God's spokesman, for this is what the word prophet basically means, and God's spokesman not merely to his own friends or neighbours or even to his own countrymen, but "to the nations". By Jeremiah's time his people were deeply involved in the power politics of the ancient Near East. Decisions taken in Babylon and Egypt affected the lives of ordinary people in Jerusalem; and decisions taken by the Jerusalem Pentagon had repercussions in Babylon and Egypt. Jeremiah's message, therefore, had to have relevance far beyond the narrow boundaries of his own people.

The description of Jeremiah as "a prophet to the nations", however, is not so much a sign of political realism as a claim that the God in whose name Jeremiah speaks is not merely the God of Judah, but the God of the whole world, the God under whose sovereignty all decisions of power politics are taken. Any other faith would have had little relevance to Jeremiah's day, and none to ours. It was to be part of Jeremiah's ministry to challenge all views that sought to limit the power and sovereignty of the Lord, whether by confining him within the walls of a church building (see chapter 7) or by making him serve the interests of one nation which claimed to be his people. There were plenty of people in Jeremiah's day—as there are plenty in ours—only too willing to use God for their own personal or national interests (14:13ff.; ch. 28). Jeremiah was called to be used by the God who is the lord of all nations, and he believed that this was also the calling of any nation claiming to be the people of God.

HOW IT BEGAN: THE RESPONSE AND THE
REASSURANCE

Jeremiah 1:4–10 (*cont'd*)

(2) There is secondly *the prophet's response*. Characteristically we find here a response of hesitation, indeed of dismay: "Ah, Lord God!" (verse 6), as if Jeremiah were saying, "Look, God, you are making a tragic mistake, you've picked the wrong person". The reason for this hesitation?—a young man painfully aware of his own lack of experience: "I do not know how to speak, for I am only a youth" (verse 6). The word translated "youth" covers a wide age range in the Old Testament, from a newborn child to a man on the threshold of marriage. It may indicate that Jeremiah was still a teenager. Jeremiah is not here protesting, as Moses did in similar circumstances (Exod.

4:10–16), that he is not a good public speaker. His hesitation is much more fundamental than that. He feels he is being pitch-forked into a task for which he is totally unprepared and wholly inexperienced. He is overwhelmed by a sense of his own personal inadequacy. This was to be a recurring struggle in Jeremiah's life. We shall see in his "personal diary" further evidence of this tension between his own estimate of his ability and resources and the demands God made upon him. Perhaps only those who shrink from facing up to God's demands are exempt from this experi-ence. He was right. If he were being called to go it alone, he would be better not to begin the journey.

(3) There is finally *a word of reassurance*. Jeremiah's objec-tions are countered in verses 7–10. He is charged to look beyond his own resources and he is given a promise; not the promise of an easy passage or of instant success, but the promise which runs through the Old Testament and is confirmed in the New, the promise of God's continuing and dependable presence, "I am with you to deliver you" (see Exod. 3:12; Matt. 28:20). Mission impossible?—not with the one who is there in the co-pilot's seat! Not only is he not being asked to go it alone; he is not being asked to give his own mature views on the state of the nation and the church in his own day. His message is God-given.

It is likely that in the words "the Lord put forth his hand and touched my mouth" (verse 9) there is being described some supranormal intensely personal religious experience, a trance or ecstatic experience in which quite literally Jeremiah felt his mouth being touched. We must not try to eliminate the abnormal or the supranormal from the lives of the Old Testament prophets. They experienced, they did, they said strange things. The prophets, however, do not see such religious experience as an end in itself. They do not try to withdraw from everyday life to be at one with God. The experience sends them back into the world with a new mission. This is the way in which God's word comes to the prophet. So the touch on the mouth is Jeremiah's assurance that he is receiving a word from the Lord. Hence-forth he is to be God's mouthpiece.

The message given to Jeremiah is double-edged; *destructive* "to pluck up and to break down, to destroy and to overthrow", and *constructive* "to build and to plant" (verse 10). The prophets have some sharply critical things to say, but they are not by nature pessimists, nor do they enjoy preaching "hell-fire and damnation". They are realists. They know that before Israel can be set free to fulfil her destiny as the people of God in the world, there has got to be a clearing away of the debris of a misleading understanding of God. There are social and religious practices which are blinding the people to the meaning of true obedience: they must go. False securities must be undermined before true faith can be nurtured. One of the things which marks off the true prophet from the false is that he never says "All is well" when all is not well (6:14). But he never destroys for the sake of destroying; he destroys in order to prepare the way for rebuilding.

TRUE
FALSE

There is one further thing to notice about this account of the making of a prophet. When the book of Deuteronomy looks forward to the coming of a prophet like Moses it says:

> I will raise up for them a prophet like you from among their brethren; and I will put my words in his mouth, and he shall speak to them all that I command him. (Deut. 18:18)

This is very like "Behold, I have put my words in your mouth" (verse 9) and "whatever I command you you shall speak" (verse 7). Likewise the promise made to Jeremiah in verse 8 echoes the promise made to Moses in Exod. 3:12. Although, as we have seen, Jeremiah's excuse for hesitating to respond to God's call is somewhat different from that of Moses—Moses indeed had a whole battery of excuses—there are other indications in the book (e.g. 15:1–4) which suggest that throughout Jeremiah is being portrayed as a new Moses. Just as Moses once led his people to freedom from enslavement in Egypt, so it was to be the painful task of Jeremiah to call his people to a new freedom from enslavement to much that mistakenly they believed to be essential to their faith. Just as Moses was there when the Lord bound himself to his people in a covenant, so Jeremiah was to hold out the hope of a new covenant (31:31–34).

TWO VISIONS (i)

Jeremiah 1:11–19

> [11]And the word of the Lord came to me, saying, "Jeremiah, what do you see?" And I said, "I see a rod of almond." [12]Then the Lord said to me, "You have seen well, for I am watching over my word to perform it."
>
> [13]The word of the Lord came to me a second time, saying, "What do you see?" And I said, "I see a boiling pot, facing away from the north." [14]Then the Lord said to me, "Out of the north evil shall break forth upon all the inhabitants of the land. [15]For, lo, I am calling all the tribes of the kingdoms of the north, says the Lord; and they shall come and every one shall set his throne at the entrance of the gates of Jerusalem, against all its walls round about, and against all the cities of Judah. [16]And I will utter my judgments against them, for all their wickedness in forsaking me; they have burned incense to other gods, and worshipped the works of their own hands. [17]But you, gird up your loins; arise, and say to them everything that I command you. Do not be dismayed by them, lest I dismay you before them. [18]And I, behold, I make you this day a fortified city, an iron pillar, and bronze walls, against the whole land, against the kings of Judah, its princes, its priests, and the people of the land. [19]They will fight against you; but they shall not prevail against you, for I am with you, says the Lord, to deliver you."

The account of Jeremiah's call to be a prophet is immediately followed by two visions. It is unlikely that these visions came to Jeremiah at the same time as his call, but they touch on themes which were to be central to his experience as a prophet. The visions are of a type common enough in the Old Testament:

   (i) They centre upon a very ordinary everyday object: in the first vision in verses 11–12 an almond twig, in the second in verses 13–14 a boiling pot. A prophet does not necessarily see different things from other people, but he sees them differently.

  (ii) They involve the prophet in a question and answer session with God—"Jeremiah, what do you see?" And I said, "I see ... Then the Lord said ..."—and out of this there comes a message.

(iii) In the case of the first vision the message is triggered off by a play on words, a kind of pun. The trouble with such puns, of course, is that they tend to fall flat when they are translated from one language into another.

You will find similar visions in Amos 7:1–9 and 8:1–3.

The vision of the "rod of almond" or an almond twig (verses 11–12) touches upon what to the prophet was a deeply personal question, and one which is never far from the heart of all true faith. The almond tree, Hebrew *shaqed*, is the first tree to burst into white blossom after the apparent deadness of the winter months. It is the sign of the coming spring. The sight of such a *shaqed* triggers off in Jeremiah's mind the conviction that God is *shoqed* "watching", "watching over my word to perform it" or, as the NEB renders, "early on the watch to carry out my purpose". A prophet stakes everything on this conviction that God is in control, that he is carrying out his purpose in the world. But how can he be sure? There were many people in Jeremiah's day, as there are many in ours, who think otherwise. The prophet Zephaniah, a slightly older contemporary of Jeremiah, speaks of people in Jerusalem who say: "The Lord will not do good, nor will he do ill" (Zeph. 1:12). In other words God will do nothing, he is powerless.

Jeremiah was to have a personal problem of this kind. If, in 627 B.C., he began preaching a word of judgement soon to come upon his people, twenty years later there were few, if any, signs of its coming. Indeed a mood of increasingly self-confident optimism prevailed in Jerusalem. For all the effect his preaching had had, he might as well have kept his breath to cool his porridge. There were those who openly ridiculed the prophet and sarcastically said to him, "Where is the word of the Lord? Let it come!" (17:15). The only assurance that it would come was this conviction that, whatever the appearances to the contrary, God was still in control. It was not a conviction that Jeremiah found easy to live with. There were, as we shall see, dark days of doubt, when Jeremiah wondered whether God was still in control and whether life had any meaning. But if this conviction had finally gone, all would have been lost; without it there can be no continuing faith.

TWO VISIONS (ii)

Jeremiah 1:11–19 (*cont'd*)

The second vision (verses 13–14) is concerned with the content of the message which the prophet has to deliver. Although some of the detail in verse 13 is not entirely clear, its general meaning is. On a blazing fire fanned by the wind there is a "boiling pot". It is tilted away from the north, so that its scalding contents spill out southwards. This is a picture of trouble brewing for the people of Judah and Jerusalem. It was from the north that such trouble usually came in Old Testament times, in the shape of invaders, whether they be Aramaeans, Assyrians, or in Jeremiah's time the Babylonians. The vision, and the expanded reference in verse 15 to "all the tribes of the kingdoms of the north", or perhaps better "all the peoples of the north and their kings", do not clearly identify this northern peril. As Jeremiah's ministry progressed, however, it became ever more clear that the foe from the north was to be identified with the neo-Babylonian empire and its imperialistic ambitions which dominated the politics of the Middle East towards the end of the seventh century B.C.

This message of impending disaster was hardly designed to be a popular word for the day. It would not gain Jeremiah honorary membership of the officers' club in the Jerusalem Pentagon; nor make him an acceptable member of the Jerusalem Temple ministers' fraternal, whose proceedings might well have begun with the hearty singing of Psalm 48 with its confident assertion that Jerusalem was "the city of our God, which God establishes for ever" (Ps. 48:8).

But Jeremiah was not courting popularity, nor was he concerned merely with the political future of his nation. He saw his nation as "the people of God" bound to God in a relationship which the Old Testament often describes by the word "covenant". This relationship was founded on the grace and the promises of God, but it demanded from the people a responsive obedience. Such obedience and loyalty Jeremiah found sadly lacking in the community of his day. They were in breach of the covenant. Instead of having "no other gods" (Exod. 20:3), they had "burned incense" (verse 16) or offered sacrifices to other gods: instead of having "no images" (Exod. 20:4), they had worshipped before the symbols of alien gods, symbols which they had made with their own hands. They were therefore under God's judgement, subject to the curses which are the consequence of disobedience to God's demands (see Deut. 27:15ff.). The yardsticks by which most people measure national or personal greatness and success are irrelevant to the prophet; he is only interested in God's yardstick.

The concluding verses of the chapter (verses 17–19) return to and develop ideas which appear in the earlier verses dealing with the prophet's call. They contain in verse 17, (a) a *renewed challenge*, "gird up your loins", i.e. gather up the long, flowing garment you are wearing, tie it round your waist that you may move freely; or as we would say, "strip for action". For the prophet such action meant being faithful to the word God had given him at whatever cost. Then comes (b) *a warning*, which might be better translated, "Don't be nervous because of them, or I will make you lose your nerve in front of them". It sounds a harsh warning; but it is realistic. The prophet's ministry is going to be difficult. If he panics when faced with opposition then his ministry is finished, and he will soon be totally discredited. Finally, in verse 19, there is (c) *a promise*. The language used in this promise, which concludes with the same words as verse 8, is predominantly military. It points clearly to the struggle that lies ahead, a struggle with the political and religious establishment as well as with the majority of his fellow-citizens. The going would be tough, but the resources more than adequate. However strong and violent the opposition it would not prevail.

We have spent some time on this opening chapter of the book of Jeremiah since whoever put it into its present shape rightly saw that it would stand as an introduction to the rest of the book. It touches upon themes which, with many a variation, are to be heard again and again in the succeeding chapters.

B. GOD'S PEOPLE—IN THE WRONG AND ON THE WAY TO DISASTER (CHS. 2–6)

GOD'S PEOPLE IN THE WRONG

Jeremiah 2:1–6:30

With chapter 2 we begin a section of the book (chapters 2–6) which contains a collection of usually brief passages illustrating the major themes in Jeremiah's preaching. Much of it may come from the earliest period of the prophet's ministry prior to the reformation of 621 B.C., though in its present form it comes from a later date. The themes are played and replayed in different keys and with many variations that are not always apparent in English translation. In chapter 2, for example, "you" is singular and feminine in verses 2–3, 14–19, 20–28, 33ff., while the "you" of verses 4–13 and 29–32 is masculine and plural. If when you read these chapters you find a good deal of repetition, remember this is the record of a prophet's preaching. He has—as all good preachers have—a limited number of themes. He sounds them again and again with urgency and passion. Among these themes three stand out.

(1) The people are *"in the wrong" with God*. They themselves may be blind to this fact, they may wish to protest their innocence (e.g. 2:35), but to the prophet the evidence points to only one verdict, guilty, guilty on two counts:

   (i) Committed to being loyal to one God, the Lord, who had made them into a nation and given them their identity, the people had compromised this loyalty by joining in the worship of other gods, particularly the Baals, the local fertility gods of the land of Canaan; and

   (ii) injustice, corruption, social evils of many kinds were rampant within the community.

These two things are not unrelated. They are the opposite sides of the one coin. There are those who say that it does not matter what we call God or how we worship him so long as we are at heart religious. To this Jeremiah, and all the Old Testament prophets would reply: it does matter; <u>all religions are not the same either with respect to the character of the god who is worshipped or in terms of the impact belief and worship make upon the life of the worshipper</u>.

To a nation whose life was deeply bound to the soil, as Israel's was after the settlement in Canaan, it made sense to worship the god or gods of the soil, the gods who guaranteed continuing fertility, abundant harvests and hence the prosperity of the community. In Canaan there were such farmers' gods, notably Baal, the god of the storm-cloud and the fertilising rain, the god of life. To worship Baal in his many different local manifestations, "the Baals" (2:23), was to take out a comprehensive insurance policy for the future. It was to give so that you could receive; and this giving took many forms. The link between the fertility of the soil, mother earth, and human sexuality is obvious. One of the ways of worshipping Baal was to share in and to stimulate the life force which he represented by having intercourse at the local shrines with female devotees of the god called "holy women". Is this a sacred, holy act or is it immorality? It depends on your view of God (cf. Amos 2:7).

Many Israelites found nothing wrong in continuing to worship the Lord, the God of their fathers, and at the same time worshipping the Baals or taking over practices associated with the worship of Baal and incorporating them in the worship of the Lord. After all surely the Lord was a god of fertility, as much the lord of the harvest as Baal. But this was to forget what was central to Israel's religious tradition. The Lord had not been discovered in the scattering of the seed or at the end of a plough. He was the God who had made himself known in the events that led to the birth of a nation. He was the God who had brought his people out of enslavement in Egypt (2:6). He was the God who in the mystery of his love had taken the initiative in establishing a relationship between himself and his people, a relationship for which the Old Testament often uses the word "*covenant*". If this covenant was rooted in God's grace it was nonetheless a demanding relationship. Israel had received so that she could learn to give; to give undivided loyalty to this God, and to give expression to that loyalty in a community whose life would be characterised by "truth", "justice" and "uprightness" (see 4:2).

For such a society Jeremiah looked in vain. Without it worship was a hollow mockery. You cannot, claims Jeremiah, murder the innocent (2:34), flock to the brothels, commit adultery (5:7–8), wallow in irresponsible luxury, pervert the course of justice (5:26–27) and claim to be in the right with God. Jeremiah pulls no punches. He could not afford to. The people of his day—like most of us—were past masters in the art of being blind to their own faults. He had to destroy the complacency, the false religiosity which kept the churches packed and prevented the people from facing the cold fact that they were *in the wrong with God*.

GOD'S PEOPLE ON THE WAY TO DISASTER

Jeremiah 2:1–6:30 (*cont'd*)

The other two main themes in these chapters have to do with disaster.

(2) *Disaster is on the way*. This is the inevitable consequence of being in the wrong with God. To ignore the demands and the responsibilities of the covenant relationship is to guarantee that there will be no security, no future for the community. In a powerful poem in 4:23–24 Jeremiah depicts the breakdown in social relationships in terms of the story of creation in reverse. It is as if the reel of film containing Genesis 1 were being run backwards. The ordered world returns to primordial chaos, light vanishes into darkness, life disappears. It is a picture of total and utter destruction. Jeremiah makes clear that it is the people themselves who make this inevitable:

> Your ways and your doings
>   have brought this upon you.
> This is your doom, and it is bitter;
>   it has reached your very heart. (4:18)

The agent of this doom is described as evil or disaster coming from the north—the development of the theme of the second vision in 1:13–14. The description is that of an invading army, horses and chariots (4:13), bow and spear (6:23), siege operations (4:16; 6:6). The identity of this northern invader is not given. Perhaps early in his ministry Jeremiah neither knew nor cared. It was enough to know that God was at the centre and in control of the swiftly moving events of the day, and through them was bringing well-merited judgement upon his people.

(3) *Disaster is on the way but it has not yet come.* There is, therefore, still time to repent, time to do a right about-turn, to change direction, to walk towards God instead of away from him. This is the theme of a series of passages in 3:1–4:4 which play on different meanings of the Hebrew word *shuv*, "to turn" or "to return". Jeremiah is seeking to bring his people to the point of decision. They have choices to make. There can be no easy or superficial repentance, but a return to God is still possible, and the conditions for such a genuine return are clearly spelled out (4:1–2). "Choose", says Jeremiah to his people. In the early days of his ministry he seems to have been sustained by the hope that they would choose life rather than death. It was to be a fading hope.

These then are the leading themes in chapters 2–6, but before we look at them more closely let us remember that we are dealing, in the main, with poetry. It is not calm, reflective poetry, but the passionate outpouring of a poet preacher, seeking to stab a nation's conscience awake. Nevertheless it is poetry, emotionally highly-charged, full of the vivid imagery of a poet sensitive to much that he sees around him in town and country. To read it as if it were "A Plain Man's Guide to the Religious Life" is to kill it or, worse, to misunderstand it.

In particular, sexual imagery abounds in these chapters. In 2:2f. the relationship between God and Israel is thought of as a marriage, the honeymoon period in the marriage. In 2:5 God, speaking like a hurt lover, asks, "What have I done wrong?" Over and over again the worship of the fertility gods of Canaan is described as "seeking lovers" (2:33) or "playing the harlot with many lovers" (3:1). In 3:2 we find the Old Testament equivalent of "walking the streets" (cf. 5:7). Sometimes English translations shy away from an obscene word or phrase. Thus in 2:20 the Good News Bible politely paraphrases "you worshipped fertility gods"; the NEB comes nearer the original with "you sprawled in promiscuous vice"! The people's lust for other gods is compared in 2:24 to that of a wild she-ass, scenting the urine of a male, and careering off in pursuit to satisfy her desires. It is as well not to be too prudish if you wish to understand the Bible.

A STRANGE CASE OF INFIDELITY (i)

Jeremiah 2:1–13

¹The word of the Lord came to me, saying, ²"Go and proclaim in the hearing of Jerusalem, Thus says the Lord,
I remember the devotion of your youth,
    your love as a bride,
how you followed me in the wilderness,
    in a land not sown.
³Israel was holy to the Lord,
    the first fruits of his harvest.
All who ate of it became guilty;
    evil came upon them,
                    says the Lord."

⁴Hear the word of the Lord, O house of Jacob, and all the families of the house of Israel. ⁵Thus says the Lord:
"What wrong did your fathers find in me
    that they went far from me,
and went after worthlessness, and became worthless?
⁶They did not say, 'Where is the Lord
    who brought us up from the land of Egypt,
who led us in the wilderness,
    in a land of deserts and pits,
in a land of drought and deep darkness,
    in a land that none passes through,
    where no man dwells?'

⁷And I brought you into a plentiful land
    to enjoy its fruits and its good things.
But when you came in you defiled my land,
    and made my heritage an abomination.
⁸The priests did not say, 'Where is the Lord?'
    Those who handle the law did not know me;
the rulers transgressed against me;
    the prophets prophesied by Baal,
    and went after things that do not profit.

⁹"Therefore I still contend with you,
                                 says the Lord,
    and with your children's children I will contend.
¹⁰For cross to the coasts of Cyprus and see,
    or send to Kedar and examine with care;
    see if there has been such a thing.
¹¹Has a nation changed its gods,
    even though they are no gods?
But my people have changed their glory
    for that which does not profit.
¹²Be appalled, O heavens, at this,
    be shocked, be utterly desolate,
                                 says the Lord,
¹³for my people have committed two evils:
    they have forsaken me,
the fountain of living waters,
    and hewed out cisterns for themselves,
broken cisterns,
    that can hold no water."

Here is a story with which we are only too sadly familiar today,
the story of a marriage gone wrong. This picture of a marriage to
describe the relationship between God and Israel is one of the
many signs that Jeremiah is deeply indebted to a prophet of a
century earlier, the prophet Hosea (see Hos. 1–3). It had begun
so promisingly. In the honeymoon period the people's attitude to
the Lord was one of *devotion*, Hebrew *hesed* (verse 2). This
Hebrew word has a rich variety of meanings. The RSV often
translates "steadfast love". Constancy and fidelity are of its
essence; the attitude that keeps husband and wife together when

it would be easier for one or the other to walk out. Strong and secure in the knowledge that she belonged to the Lord, Israel was *holy* (see comment on 1:5). Just as at harvest time the people had to bring "some of the first of all the fruit of the ground which you harvest" (Deut. 26:2) and offer it to the Lord, the sign that all that they had was his gift, so Israel was the first fruit of the Lord's harvest (verse 3).

Then the marriage began to turn sour. A bond, forged and tested in the harsh life of the desert, snapped with the coming of prosperity in the land of Canaan (2:6–7). To the people, the gods of the soil proved more attractive and less demanding partners than the Lord who had brought them out of Egypt. To the wronged, divine husband it is all so bewildering. Does his wife not know that she is on a course that can only lead to disillusionment? The people ". . . went after worthlessness and became worthless" (verse 5).There is heavy sarcasm here and a play on the Hebrew word *hebel*, the word which occurs frequently in the book of Ecclesiastes where it is traditionally translated "vanity". It points to something insubstantial like a puff of wind, or as we might say "mere hot air" or "a will o' the wisp". But this word *hebel* sounds something like the name of the Canaanite fertility god Baal (pronounced with two syllables), and *baal* is also one of the Hebrew words for husband. John Bright in the Anchor Bible gets the flavour of this by translating

And following Lord Delusion,
  Deluded became.

Jeremiah never ceases to be amazed that his people are prepared to settle for a delusion, when they have known the truth, and the truth can still be theirs. This is the point of an arresting picture in verse 13. In a land with uncertain annual rainfall the very life and prosperity of a community depends upon an adequate and dependable supply of water. What better than a constant spring of fresh running water? Lacking such a spring, water has to be stored in cisterns hollowed out of the porous limestone rocks. To prevent the water seeping away, such cisterns had to be lined with plaster. If the plaster cracked the cistern would soon empty. Come to such a cistern looking for life-sustaining water and you look in vain. That, says Jeremiah, is what these other superficially attractive gods are, cracked, empty cisterns. What a strange sense of values, to exchange the Lord, a dependable spring of life-giving water, for such cracked empty cisterns. It is easy to look back and say "Of course Jeremiah was right; how could the people be so blind?"; it is far more difficult to face honestly those substitutes for the living God which we place at the centre of our lives, substitutes which can only prove to be pathetically inadequate.

A STRANGE CASE OF INFIDELITY (ii)

Jeremiah 2:1–13 (*cont'd*)

For Israel, however, there was one extenuating circumstance. This was a case of a people misled by those who ought to have known better. In verse 8 we find the first of Jeremiah's many bitter attacks on the religious and political leadership of his day (cf. 5:13, 30–31; 6:13–15; 14:18; 23:9ff.). Three groups are singled out for condemnation:

(1) *The priests*. We tend to think of the priests in Israel as being primarily concerned with offering sacrifices, but they had a far wider and more important function. They are described as "those who handle the law" (verse 8). They had a teaching ministry within the community, being responsible for handing on from generation to generation, and interpreting to the people, *torah*, the law, God's revelation of himself, his will and his purposes. But, says the prophet, the blind were claiming to lead the blind; the teachers themselves needed taught. They "did not know" the Lord. Such knowledge was no mere head knowledge, but the personal commitment to God which would lead to a life of obedience (see Hos. 4:1ff.).

(2) *The rulers* (Hebrew "shepherds"). Shepherd is a well-known title for king in the ancient Near East and Israel. The king

was no mere figurehead in Israel. He had a key role to play in the religious and political life of the people. Upon the character and decisions of the king the well-being of the community depended. Psalm 72 sketches a picture of what is expected from a true king. Instead of dealing justly and fairly, however, and defending the cause of the poor and the needy, kings in Israel often played the irresponsible despot; instead of seeing themselves as the servants of the Lord, they often rebelled against the Lord. You will see what Jeremiah thinks of one such king in 22:13–19.

(3) *The prophets*. Jeremiah was dogged all his life by other prophets, claiming as he did to speak the word of the Lord, and delivering a message which was much more acceptable to the people, and which contradicted much of what he said. This raised serious questions which are touched upon elsewhere in the Old Testament (see for example the stories in 1 Kings chapters 13 and 22). Faced with conflicting voices, claiming to speak with equal certainty and sincerity in the name of God, how do people know which is the true word of the Lord? How does a prophet himself know that the word he preaches is authentic? How do we know? We shall find ourselves coming back again and again to such questions in our study of Jeremiah. Here it is said "the prophets prophesied by Baal" (verse 8); like the people they found the worship of Baal more exciting and stimulating than the worship of the Lord. In the phrase "and went after things that do not profit" there is a play on the name Baal and the Hebrew for "and do not profit"—it occurs again in verse 11. It is impossible to render this into English, but perhaps we get the flavour of what Jeremiah is saying if we think of these prophets of Baal as playing a profitless game.

The marriage has gone wrong: the faithless wife now finds herself in the law court:

> Therefore I still contend with you, says the Lord,
>   and with your children's children I will contend. (verse 9)

The word translated "contend" (Hebrew *riv*) is a legal word which indicates that the Lord has a charge to bring against his people. Indeed the whole of chapter 2 can be read as the transcript of a court case. The Lord is the plaintiff. He accuses his people of blatant infidelity; he itemises their crimes and, as we shall see, like a skilful prosecuting counsel anticipates and dismisses their plea of innocence. This is a case, claims the plaintiff (verses 10–12), astonishing and unparalleled in its enormity. Go west to the islands of the Mediterranean, for example Cyprus; east to the desert communities, for example Kedar; search the whole wide world and see if any other nation has exchanged its gods. How ironic that Israel, to whom had been given the privilege of knowing the majesty and splendour of the one true God, should outpagan the pagans, replacing this God with gods who are no gods! We are sometimes told that the ways of God are strange; the ways of people can be even more strange.

THE INNOCENT AND THE GUILTY

Jeremiah 2:14–19

14"Is Israel a slave? Is he a homeborn servant?
    Why then has he become a prey?
15The lions have roared against him,
    they have roared loudly.
They have made his land a waste;
    his cities are in ruins, without inhabitant.
16Moreover, the men of Memphis and Tahpanhes
    have broken the crown of your head.
17Have you not brought this upon yourself
    by forsaking the Lord your God,
    when he led you in the way?
18And now what do you gain by going to Egypt,
    to drink the waters of the Nile?
Or what do you gain by going to Assyria,
    to drink the waters of the Euphrates?
19Your wickedness will chasten you,
    and your apostasy will reprove you.

> Know and see that it is evil and bitter
>   for you to forsake the Lord your God;
>   the fear of me is not in you,
>   says the Lord God of hosts."

This passage seems to anticipate a possible argument for the defence. If the Lord really is our husband, why has he not protected us? Many a time the people had seen their countryside devastated, their cities sacked by invaders. In 722 B.C. the Assyrians, often depicted as a lion (verse 15), had destroyed the northern kingdom of Israel. Judah survived for over a century, but only by being for much of the time a compliant vassal state in the Assyrian empire. In 609 B.C. a bid for national renewal and independence under King Josiah met with disaster. Judah, for a brief period before the Babylonians took over, was at the mercy of the Egyptians—Memphis and Tahpanhes, mentioned in verse 16, were important Egyptian towns. In the light of this, would not slavery (verse 14)—whether being sold as a slave or being born into a slave family—be a better description of the nation's condition than marriage to the Lord?

In difficult times there were those who saw the answer to Judah's problems in terms of political expediency; hence the pro Assyrian and the pro-Egyptian lobbies in Jerusalem (verse 18). To Jeremiah, however, Judah was not merely another nation whose future could be guaranteed by skilfully playing the game of power politics. Judah was the people of God; her problems and her destiny were religious. There is no point, he claims, in blaming God for what has happened. The Lord has done nothing wrong; it is you, your wickedness, your infidelity which has led and will lead to disaster (verses 17, 19). A scapegoat, not least a divine scapegoat, can be very comforting. Forget it, says Jeremiah, the buck stops right here ... with you.

The way in which people talk about God can be very revealing. Twice in this section we find God described as "the Lord your God" (verses 17, 19) and once as "the Lord God of hosts" (verse 19). The Lord of hosts is a traditional title for God in the Old Testament. Its original meaning is possibly best seen in the story of David and Goliath, where David defiantly says to Goliath, "I come to you in the name of the Lord of hosts, the God of the armies of Israel, whom you have defied" (1 Sam. 17:45). This is the God of Israel's far-flung battle line. Perhaps for many people in Israel the phrase always had a strongly patriotic and nationalistic flavour. This fits in with its use in Psalms such as Psalm 46 which speak of God protecting his people against all their enemies:

> The Lord of hosts is with us;
>   the God of Jacob is our refuge. (Ps. 46:7, 11)

In other Old Testament passages, however, and especially in the prophets, the hosts came to mean not only the armies of Israel but all the forces in the universe under God's control. When Jeremiah uses the phrase "the Lord of hosts"—and he often does—it is usually in passages which speak of judgement upon God's people and coming disaster. To say "the Lord of hosts is with you" is dangerous; the power of God, in which you seek protection, may in certain circumstances round upon you and destroy. To speak of "the Lord your God" is to confess that you belong to God, not that God belongs to you—there is a difference. Sometimes we speak too easily and reassuringly of the love of God, forgetting that nothing is as inexorable as love, nothing more demanding.

A PEOPLE'S TRAGEDY AND DESPERATE PLIGHT

Jeremiah 2:20–28

> ²⁰"For long ago you broke your yoke
>   and burst your bonds;
>   and you said, 'I will not serve.'
> Yea, upon every high hill
>   and under every green tree
>   you bowed down as a harlot.
> ²¹Yet I planted you a choice vine,
>   wholly of pure seed.
> How then have you turned degenerate

and become a wild vine?
²²Though you wash yourself with lye
  and use much soap,
  the stain of your guilt is still before me,

says the Lord God.

²³How can you say, 'I am not defiled,
  I have not gone after the Baals'?
Look at your way in the valley;
  know what you have done—
a restive young camel interlacing her tracks,
²⁴ a wild ass used to the wilderness,
  in her heat sniffing the wind!
    Who can restrain her lust?
None who seek her need weary themselves;
  in her month they will find her.
²⁵Keep your feet from going unshod
  and your throat from thirst.
But you said, 'It is hopeless,
  for I have loved strangers,
  and after them I will go.'

²⁶"As a thief is shamed when caught,
  so the house of Israel shall be shamed:
they, their kings, their princes,
  their priests, and their prophets,
²⁷who say to a tree, 'You are my father,'
  and to a stone, 'You gave me birth.'
For they have turned their back to me,
  and not their face.
But in the time of their trouble they say,
  'Arise and save us!'
²⁸But where are your gods
  that you made for yourself?
Let them arise, if they can save you,
  in your time of trouble;
for as many as your cities
  are your gods, O Judah."

The case for the prosecution continues. In a series of metaphors the tragedy of the people's break with God and its dire consequences are spelled out. In the first section (verses 20–22) the people are compared to (a) a runaway animal refusing to return to its master; (b) a prostitute plying her trade at the shrines, or high places, associated with the worship of the fertility gods; (c) a choice vine that strangely grows wild and so produces useless grapes (cf. Isa. ch. 5).

There is no easy solution, no known detergent on the market which can remove this stain, the stain of guilt and of that deep-seated perversion that runs through the people's life. The defence plea of innocence is then rejected (verses 23–25) by pointing to the evidence of what has happened "in the valley". The Valley of Ben Hinnom, just outside Jerusalem, was notorious for pagan practices, including child sacrifice (Jer. 7:21–26; 2 Kings 23:10). It is a measure of how deeply addicted the people are that they see nothing wrong in such practices. Evil brings its own distorted sense of values.

The faithlessness of the people is then described in two pictures: (a) that of the young camel, skittish, unsteady on its feet, dashing off, now in one direction now in the other: (b) that of the she-ass in heat, sniffing the urine of the male, careering after a mate; no need to chase her, she does the chasing. So the people have only too eagerly run after other gods. Then comes the warning: conduct like this can only end in exhaustion. But the warning falls on deaf ears. The people are hooked; like a drug addict, aware of the possible dangers in the situation, yet unable to stifle the craving for another shot.

We tend to deplore half-empty churches and the decline in religion. That was not the prophet's problem. Religion in his day was big business, but it was the great illusion. The streets of the cities were chock-a-block with the images and symbols of gods (verses 26–28). But when the day of crisis comes such gods will turn out to be wholly powerless, unable to lift a finger to help their ardent worshippers. Like a thief caught red-handed, they will discover to their shame that their religion is a meaningless charade. The *tree*, referred to in verse 27, is probably the *asherah* or sacred pole, symbol of the Canaanite fertility goddess, Asherah, the mother of Baal; the *stone*, the *matsevah* or standing pillar, the representation of the male fertility god.

There is savage mockery in Jeremiah's words—these poor, confused people saying to the symbol of a goddess, "you are my
father", and to the symbol of a god, "you are my mother". But
this is no more than a reflection of a deeper and more serious
confusion, the failure to see the difference between the one true
living God and the lifeless substitutes which have misled them.

FACE THE FACTS

Jeremiah 2:29–37

29"Why do you complain against me?
　　You have all rebelled against me,
　　　　　　　　　　　　　　says the Lord.
30In vain have I smitten your children,
　　they took no correction;
　your own sword devoured your prophets
　　like a ravening lion.
31And you, O generation, heed the word of the Lord.
　Have I been a wilderness to Israel,
　　or a land of thick darkness?
　Why then do my people say, 'We are free,
　　we will come no more to thee'?
32Can a maiden forget her ornaments,
　　or a bride her attire?
　Yet my people have forgotten me
　　days without number.

33"How well you direct your course
　　to seek lovers!
　So that even to wicked women
　　you have taught your ways.
34Also on your skirts is found
　　the lifeblood of guiltless poor;
　you did not find them breaking in.
　　Yet in spite of all these things
35you say, 'I am innocent;
　　surely his anger has turned from me.'
　Behold, I will bring you to judgment
　　for saying, 'I have not sinned.'

³⁶How lightly you gad about,
　　changing your way!
You shall be put to shame by Egypt
　　as you were put to shame by Assyria.
³⁷From it too you will come away
　　with your hands upon your head,
for the Lord has rejected those in whom you trust,
　　and you will not prosper by them."

In spite of all protestations of innocence (verse 35), the case for the defence is non-existent. The verdict must be guilty, guilty of rebellion against God. Why then continue the case? This is the meaning of the opening words of verse 29, where the word translated in the RSV "complain" is the same legal word translated "contend" in verse 9. There are not even any mitigating circumstances. The lesson of the past when Israel had felt the heavy hand of God's judgement had been ignored: witness Amos 4:6–11 with its series of warnings and its recurring, poignant refrain "yet you did not return to me".

The prophets who ought to have been listened to as God's messengers had not only been ignored; they had been liquidated (verse 30). There is at least one authenticated case of this happening to a prophetic contemporary of Jeremiah; see 26:20–23; and Jeremiah himself was lucky not to suffer a similar fate; see chapter 37. The true prophet hardly qualifies as a popular preacher. If popularity be the test, then the verdict on the ministry of every one of the great prophetic figures in the Old Testament must be failure. We look back and with hindsight say, "yes, that was the true word of God", but the prophet's contemporaries were more likely to crucify him, with indifference if in no other way; and this was Jesus' experience too.

In spite of the Lord's continuing goodness—has he ever been inhospitable to you? argues verse 31—the people decided astonishingly to do their own thing, freed, so they thought, from the shackles the Lord had placed upon them. Doing their own thing led to a horrifying catalogue of misdeeds:

(1) a rampant religious enthusiasm which led the people to offer their services so blatantly to the fertility deities that they

could have taught a professional prostitute a thing or two (verse 33).

(2) social anarchy, symbolised by the murder of poor, innocent people without any semblance of legality. The words "you did not find them breaking in" in verse 34 refers to the law in Exod. 22:2-3 which regards killing a burglar caught breaking in at night as justifiable homicide.

(3) political expediency, trying to play the game of power politics, which could only lead to national disaster; "your hands upon your head" (verse 37) is one of the recognised signs of mourning (see 2 Sam. 13:19). Such were the fruits of "freedom". By implication the only true freedom for the people of God is that freedom which is found in commitment to God, a commitment which must find expression in every aspect of life, in personal decisions and in the way the community chooses its priorities. For such a commitment Jeremiah repeatedly pleaded.

IS RECONCILIATION POSSIBLE?

Jeremiah 3:1-5

¹"If a man divorces his wife
   and she goes from him
and becomes another man's wife,
   will he return to her?
Would not that land be greatly polluted?
You have played the harlot with many lovers;
   and would you return to me?
                says the Lord.
²Lift up your eyes to the bare heights, and see!
   Where have you not been lain with?
By the waysides you have sat awaiting lovers
   like an Arab in the wilderness.
You have polluted the land
   with your vile harlotry.
³Therefore the showers have been withheld,
   and the spring rain has not come;
yet you have a harlot's brow,

you refuse to be ashamed.
⁴Have you not just now called to me,
  'My father, thou art the friend of my youth—
⁵will he be angry for ever,
  will he be indignant to the end?'
Behold, you have spoken,
  but you have done all the evil that you could."

A broken marriage, a faithless, guilty wife . . . is that the end of the story, or is a new beginning possible, and if so, on what terms? This is the theme of a series of passages gathered together in 3:1–4:4. Although not all of this material can with certainty be attributed to Jeremiah—this is particularly true of the prose section in 3:16–18, and to a lesser extent of 3:6–11—there is no doubt that reconciliation based on the call to "turn", Hebrew *shuv*, was an important element in Jeremiah's early preaching.

This word *shuv* throbs like an insistent motif throughout the passages; forms of the word occur no less than eighteen times, a fact concealed by English translations. It has several meanings all derived from the basic idea of turning. You can turn in different directions. You can turn away from someone, turning your back on them, deserting them; so a noun from the verb *shuv* is used to describe Israel as "the faithless one" in 3:6,8,11,12. You can turn back or turn towards someone, so the word is used in the sense of returning, of doing that right about-turn, back to God, which is what the Bible means by repenting; this is the meaning it has in 3:22; 4:1. There is a play on these different meanings in the phrase translated "Return, faithless Israel" in 3:12, and in the similar phrase in 3:14 and 3:22 "Return, O faithless children/sons". Perhaps we catch something of the flavour of this if we translate 3:12 "Turn back, turn-coat Israel". Let us look now at the various kinds of "turning" of which the passages speak.

To understand the first of them in 3:1–5 we have got to look at an old law preserved in Deut. 24:1–4. It deals with divorce, and stipulates that when a woman is legally divorced and remarries, then if her second husband divorces her or dies, her first may not under any circumstances take her again to be his wife. Such a practice would be repulsive to the Lord, and would bring guilt upon the land. But are not the people of Israel in a worse plight? They have not remarried once; they have played fast and loose with many lovers. How then can they expect to return, to be reconciled to the Lord, their first husband? Legally it is impossible. What then is the point of this illustration? It seems to be saying two things:

(1) It is trying to make the people face honestly the difficulties in the way of reconciliation. True reconciliation, as we well know in human relationships, is a difficult, costly experience, which can never be built on a quick "let's forget it" attitude. A faithless, unrepentant people cannot simply turn to God as if he were some benign sugar daddy, momentarily angry but at heart a soft, indulgent friend prepared to give them anything they ask as soon as they say "please". Reconciliation can never be merely a matter of words.

(2) It is pointing to reconciliation based, not on what is legally possible, but on something which goes beyond the law or any legal rights the people may or may not have, to that something in the character of God which alone can give hope of a new beginning. The Old Testament too is the story of a prodigal and of reconciliation flowing from the unchanging, costly love of a father. Perhaps this is best said in another prophetic book where God addresses a broken, despairing people and says:

> Can a woman forget her sucking child,
>> that she should have no compassion on the son of her womb?
> Even these may forget,
>> yet I will not forget you. (Isa. 49:15)

We can have no claim on such a God, we can but accept his renewing grace.

SOME PEOPLE NEVER LEARN

Jeremiah 3:6–11

⁶The Lord said to me in the days of King Josiah: "Have you seen what she did, that faithless one, Israel, how she went up on every high hill

and under every green tree, and there played the harlot? ⁷And I
thought, 'After she has done all this she will return to me'; but she did
not return, and her false sister Judah saw it. ⁸She saw that for all the
adulteries of that faithless one, Israel, I had sent her away with a
decree of divorce; yet her false sister Judah did not fear, but she too
went and played the harlot. ⁹Because harlotry was so light to her, she
polluted the land, committing adultery with stone and tree. ¹⁰Yet for
all this her false sister Judah did not return to me with her whole heart,
but in pretence, says the Lord."

¹¹And the Lord said to me, "Faithless Israel has shown herself less
guilty than false Judah."

Here is a little sermon on how to ignore the lesson of the past. A
contrast is drawn between two sisters, one of them Israel, which
here means the northern kingdom of Israel which was overrun by
the Assyrians in 722 B.C., the other Judah, the southern kingdom
which survived the Assyrian onslaught. Israel had played fast and
loose with the Lord, had refused to return to her true husband,
and had been given a divorce decree. Judah might have been
expected to learn from her sister's bitter experience. But not
a bit of it. She too played the same game, and compounded
her offence by going through the motions of returning to her
husband: she "did not return to me with her whole heart, but
in pretence [or falsely], says the Lord" (verse 10).

This statement makes most sense as a comment on the national
reformation of 621 B.C. (see commentary on 1:1–3, *The age of
crisis*). Jeremiah may at first have supported the reform movement. He was soon to be disillusioned. There was now a purified
national shrine in Jerusalem, and a continuingly corrupt people.
Outwardly much had changed; inwardly nothing had changed.
There had been a "false" return, and that was worse than no
return at all. As Jeremiah found out to his cost, there is nothing
more frustrating than trying to preach repentance to a people
who believe they have already repented. There is nothing like a
good dose of "religion" to inoculate people against the radical
claims of God.

So the verdict on Judah is "more guilty than her sister Israel".
That must have come as something of a shock to the good people

of Judah, many of whom believed that they had survived the Assyrian invasion because, in the Lord's sight, they were better than their northern apostate neighbours.

THE CALL TO RECONCILIATION

Jeremiah 3:12–18

12"Go, and proclaim these words toward the north, and say,
'Return, faithless Israel,
                        says the Lord.
I will not look on you in anger,
    for I am merciful,
                        says the Lord;
I will not be angry for ever.
13Only acknowledge your guilt,
    that you rebelled against the Lord your God
and scattered your favours among strangers under every green tree,
    and that you have not obeyed my voice,
                        says the Lord.
14Return, O faithless children,
                        says the Lord;
    for I am your master;
I will take you, one from a city and two from a family,
    and I will bring you to Zion.
15"'And I will give you shepherds after my own heart, who will feed you with knowledge and understanding. 16And when you have multiplied and increased in the land, in those days, says the Lord, they shall no more say, "The ark of the covenant of the Lord." It shall not come to mind, or be remembered, or missed; it shall not be made again. 17At that time Jerusalem shall be called the throne of the Lord, and all nations shall gather to it, to the presence of the Lord in Jerusalem, and they shall no more stubbornly follow their own evil heart. 18In those days the house of Judah shall join the house of Israel, and together they shall come from the land of the north to the land that I gave your fathers for a heritage.'"

Now comes the call for a true reconciliation. The fact that it is directed "towards the north" and is addressed to "faithless Israel" may mean that it is firstly a call to the long-scattered people of northern Israel, in whose fate Jeremiah had a continuing interest (see chapters 30–33), but it includes Judah who believed herself to be Israel in the sense of the people of God.

Two elements in true reconciliation are underlined in verses 12–13:

(1) <u>God is unchanging in his faithfulness and love</u>. The word translated "merciful" in verse 12 is the adjective corresponding to the noun translated "devotion" in 2:2 (see comment on 2:2). In this marriage the people may have been unfaithful, but not so God. His love for his erring wife has remained unchanging (see Hos. 11:8ff.). His anger may have been justified, but it cannot be his last word.

(2) From the people there must come confession, an open and honest acknowledgement of their rebellion against the Lord. <u>There can be no reconciliation unless it is based on a clear-eyed facing of the facts which led to the breakdown in the relationship.</u>

This theme of reconciliation is picked up and expanded in verses 14–18. They begin with the same call to return that we find in verse 12, a call rooted in the character of the Lord who is here described in the words "I am your master". A more literal translation would be "I am your baal". Now Baal, as we have seen, is the Canaanite god of fertility upon whom the people so freely lavished their affection; but <u>*baal* in Hebrew also means lord or master, and it is one of the words for husband.</u> So the people are being challenged to remember that their true *baal* (husband) is not Baal, but the Lord. With such a husband there is hope, the hope of a new community, its affairs wisely directed by godly rulers (shepherds).

This sober, but reassuring promise, is filled out in verses 16–18 by three pictures, each introduced by a phrase which points to a hope which will come true at some unspecified time in the future; "in those days" (verses 16,18) and "at that time" (verse 17).

(1) The first picture centres upon "the ark of the covenant", one of the earliest symbols or sacred objects in Israel's pilgrimage. It was an acacia wooden box (Exod. 25:10ff.), variously thought of as a container for the tablets on which the Ten Commandments were inscribed or as the visible throne for the invisi-

ble Lord of hosts, the God of Israel. It symbolised the presence of the Lord in the midst of his people during the period of the wandering in the wilderness and in the early battles to secure a foothold in Canaan (Num. 10:33–35; 1 Sam. ch. 4). It was eventually housed in the Holy of Holies in the Temple at Jerusalem. When it disappeared we do not know. Certainly by the time of the Babylonian capture of Jerusalem in 587 B.C. it had gone. But the symbol, however sacred, is only important as pointing to what it represents. Why bother to search for a lost ark, if it is no longer needed to reassure the people of the presence of God in their midst?

(2) The second picture (verse 17) carries on from the first. If the ark was once thought of as the throne of God it is now to be replaced by Jerusalem, a Jerusalem which will become the object of pilgrimage for all enlightened nations, since there they will find God (cf. Isa. 2:2–4).

(3) The third picture (verse 18) looks forward to the reunion of the long-divided and scattered peoples of the northern kingdom of Israel and the southern kingdom of Judah. Together they shall come to be a new people of God in the land God promised.

Some of these pictures may come to us from an age later than Jeremiah's, but they are developing the theme of hope which is central to Jeremiah's message. All of them are very down-to-earth pictures. They speak to the needs of a people at a particular time. But just as the ark of the covenant was no longer needed, so there would come a time when it was realised that the earthly city of Jerusalem was no longer essential to faith (see John 4:16–26). That is why Jerusalem becomes the new heavenly Jerusalem in the book of Revelation and the promised land is transformed into the vision of a new heaven and a new earth (Rev. chs. 21–22). The content of our visions of hope may change; but hope there must be. Without it there can be no lasting faith in a God whose faithfulness and whose loving purposes for his children must one day finally triumph.

THE ESSENTIALS FOR TRUE RECONCILIATION

Jeremiah 3:19–4:4

¹⁹"'I thought
how I would set you among my sons,
and give you a pleasant land,
a heritage most beauteous of all nations.
And I thought you would call me, My Father,
and would not turn from following me.
²⁰Surely, as a faithless wife leaves her husband,
so have you been faithless to me, O house of Israel,

says the Lord.'"

²¹A voice on the bare heights is heard,
the weeping and pleading of Israel's sons,
because they have perverted their way,
they have forgotten the Lord their God.
²²"Return, O faithless sons,
I will heal your faithlessness."
"Behold, we come to thee;
for thou art the Lord our God.
²³Truly the hills are a delusion,
the orgies on the mountains.
Truly in the Lord our God
is the salvation of Israel.
²⁴"But from our youth the shameful thing has devoured all for which our fathers laboured, their flocks and their herds, their sons and their daughters. ²⁵Let us lie down in our shame, and let our dishonour cover us; for we have sinned against the Lord our God, we and our fathers, from our youth even to this day; and we have not obeyed the voice of the Lord our God."

¹"If you return, O Israel,

says the Lord,

to me you should return.
If you remove your abominations from my presence,
and do not waver,
²and if you swear, 'As the Lord lives,'
in truth, in justice, and in uprightness,
then nations shall bless themselves in him,
and in him shall they glory."

³For thus says the Lord to the men of Judah and to the inhabitants of Jerusalem:
"Break up your fallow ground,
and sow not among thorns.
⁴Circumcise yourselves to the Lord,
remove the foreskin of your hearts,
O men of Judah and inhabitants of Jerusalem;
lest my wrath go forth like fire,
and burn with none to quench it,
because of the evil of your doings."

The marriage has ended in tragedy. The people have thrown the Lord's generosity back in his face. But infidelity brings its own bitter disillusionment. "On the bare heights", centres of the worship of the fertility gods, there is heard not the joy or gladness of worship but "the weeping and pleading of Israel's sons" (verse 21). What promised to be the good life has turned sour. The only way forward is the way back to the Lord, to seek the renewal, the healing which only he can give.

On the lips of the people we hear a liturgy of repentance and confession (verses 22b–25). It involves:

(i) a renewed pledge of loyalty to the Lord as Israel's God;
(ii) a recognition of the falseness and futility of the worship of other gods, worship which is sarcastically described as "the orgies [or the hubbub] on the mountains" (verse 23);
(iii) the acknowledgement that it is only in the Lord that true wholeness of life, help and deliverance can be found—the word "salvation" (verse 23) contains all these ideas;
(iv) a frank recognition that Israel's history has been one of continuing vitality-sapping disobedience (verses 24–25).

The "shameful thing" which destroyed the nation, is a biting lampoon on the name Baal, for which in some Old Testament texts the word "shame", Hebrew *bosheth*, is substituted—Saul, for example, according to 2 Sam. 2:8 had a son called Ishbosheth, "man of shame", a highly unlikely name for a father to give his son; 1 Chron. 8:33 gives us his real name Eshbaal. The way is open for the people to confess that participating in the worship of Baal is "our shame" (verse 25; cf. 11:13).

But liturgy must find confirmation in life: so the meaning of true repentance is spelled out in 4:1–2. It must involve not only a break with false gods, "your abominations", but a renewed loyalty to the Lord, a loyalty which will find practical expression in all that is meant by the words "truth", "justice" and "uprightness", words which are used over and over again by the prophets to describe that wholesome quality of life in a community in which the needs and rights of all men under God are recognised and met. Given such a renewal, then, through Israel other nations shall be drawn to God to find in him "blessing", a God-given richness and fulness of life. You will find a similar promise made to Abraham, Isaac and Jacob in the Genesis stories, e.g. Gen. 12:3; 18:18; 26:4. We can trace within the Old Testament a continuing tension between a narrow, nationalistic understanding of God and a wider, more catholic vision. Those who held on to the wider vision knew that such a vision placed an even greater responsibility upon Israel. Upon the life she offered to God, upon her obedience, all else depended.

So there must be a new, a radically new beginning. Any farmer knows that it makes no sense to waste good seed on a thorn-infested field. You have got to put your back into it and work to bring the rich, fallow ground into cultivation (verse 3). Nor are the outward signs of religion enough. Circumcision was the outward sign that a man belonged to the people of God. But the outward sign is meaningless, unless there is a corresponding inner reality. Hence the call to "circumcise . . . your hearts" (verse 4). Failing such an inner renewal, there can only be the grim prospect of judgement. It is this note of coming judgement upon the evil within the community which prepares the way for the next major section in the book.

COMING DISASTER AND THE REASONS FOR IT

Jeremiah 4:5–10

> [5]Declare in Judah, and proclaim in Jerusalem, and say,
> "Blow the trumpet through the land;

   cry aloud and say,
   'Assemble, and let us go
     into the fortified cities!'
   ⁶Raise a standard toward Zion,
   flee for safety, stay not,
  for I bring evil from the north,
   and great destruction.
   ⁷A lion has gone up from his thicket,
   a destroyer of nations has set out;
   he has gone forth from this place
  to make your land a waste;
   your cities will be ruins
   without inhabitant.
   ⁸For this gird you with sackcloth,
   lament and wail;
  for the fierce anger of the Lord
   has not turned back from us."

⁹"In that day, says the Lord, courage shall fail both king and princes; the priests shall be appalled and the prophets astounded." ¹⁰Then I said, "Ah, Lord God, surely thou hast utterly deceived this people and Jerusalem, saying, 'It shall be well with you'; whereas the sword has reached their very life."

These verses begin a series of variations on a common theme which continues to the end of chapter 6. Much of the material assumes that reconciliation will not, and cannot take place this side of national tragedy. The community, far from being willing to return, is stubbornly determined not to listen to any warnings (see 5:9–12, 20–24). Bitter experience probably forced Jeremiah to change the major emphasis in his preaching. "Turn" he said; and they refused to turn. There was nothing left but to say in the words of Amos, "Prepare to meet your God, O Israel!" (Amos 4:12), and to leave the people in no doubt that such a meeting would be painful.

Before we look further at 4:5–10, two general points are worth keeping in mind as we read these chapters:

(1) Here again we are dealing with a summary of some of the central issues, preached and repreached in a ministry which lasted many years. This should be clear from the way in which not

only ideas but words, verses and illustrations are repeated sometimes in different contexts. Thus 5:1–9 which focuses upon the
corruption and guilt of the community climaxes in the words:

> Shall I not punish them for these things? says the Lord;
> and shall I not avenge myself on a nation such as this? (5:9)

Exactly the same words appear in 5:29 in a section dealing with
the exploitation of the poor and those at risk in society. Several
passages attack the religious establishment of the day for encouraging a mood of complacent optimism within the community, for
example 4:9–10; 6:13–15; and this latter passage appears again in
the book in a different context in 8:10–12. To repeat home truths
is no crime. If a sermon is worth preaching once, it is worth
preaching many times. People may not have been able to recall,
or even have known, when a prophet said certain things, but the
gist of his message was remembered.

(2) We sometimes think of the prophets as the passive
messengers of God. A prophet receives a word from God; he
preaches it. His personality no more shapes the message than
the telephone does when you "Dial a prayer". In the visions in
chapter 1, however, we have already seen Jeremiah involved in a
question and answer session with God. Here, not only do we find
him laying bare the agony in his own soul (4:19–21), but in two
passages we find him in conversation with God (5:1–9; 6:9–12),
seeking new light on the message he has received, and sharing
something of his own reaction to it. Such conversations or dia-
logues with God are typical of the book of Jeremiah. It is in the
extracts from Jeremiah's "spiritual diary" that we see them in
their most revealing light, as we shall find later. But even at this
point, it is clear that the messenger does not remain unaffected by
the message he preaches.

SOUND THE ALARM

Jeremiah 4:5–10 (*cont'd*)

This is the first in a series of passages which develop the theme of
the second vision in 1:13ff., the vision of the "foe from the

north". Invasion is imminent; "Blow the trumpet" (verse 5). The trumpet, Hebrew *shophar*, is not for Israel part of a brass ensemble. It does duty for our church bells, calling people to worship, and also for the alarm bell that gives warning of an attack. What the trumpet says to the ear, the "standard" or "signal" (see 6:1), probably the fire beacon, says to the eye. Leave the indefensible villages; seek shelter in the fortified cities: the enemy comes, an enemy described as a "lion", a "destroyer of nations", in all probability the Babylonians. His intentions are clear: ruin and destruction, in face of which the community will be plunged into mourning. Yet this is not merely an enemy invasion; it is the expression of "the fierce anger of the Lord" (verse 8). The people have not turned; so the anger of the Lord *has not yet turned (shuv)* from them. Against this there is no effective defence.

Part of the blame lies with the political and religious leadership of the community and its failure to read the signs of the times (see comment on 2:8). They encouraged the people to believe that they had a secure future. "It shall be well with you" (*shalom*; verse 10), when in fact the sword was already at their throats. We are tempted to look back and say how blind, how stupid they must have been. But were they? Did they not have the best of reasons for believing that all would be well—the promises of God, promises which the past had proved to be true?

When a hundred years earlier the Assyrians had been within an ace of destroying Jerusalem the prophet Isaiah had said:

> Like birds hovering, so the Lord of hosts
>   will protect Jerusalem;
> he will protect and deliver it,
>   he will spare and rescue it. (Isa. 31:5)

And the Lord did, according to the story in 2 Kings chapter 19. Had not God made promises to the royal family of David, the promise of an everlasting covenant which would guarantee a descendant of David upon the throne in Jerusalem for all time (see 2 Sam. 7:8–16; Pss. 2 and 110)? Did not the people gather in the Temple at Jerusalem and sing:

God is our refuge and strength,
    a very present help in trouble.
Therefore we will not fear though the earth should change,
    though the mountains shake in the heart of the sea;
though its waters roar and foam,
    though the mountains tremble with its tumult.

The Lord of hosts is with us;
    the God of Jacob is our refuge. (Ps. 46:1-3, 11)

Surely this is not a God who would allow the land to become a waste, its cities ruined and uninhabited. These were deeply-held sincere convictions, and to those who held them Jeremiah's words must have seemed the words of a false prophet, a scaremonger, a heretic, a traitor to king and country. Yet Jeremiah believed such people were wrong, and that those who said "all will be well" were deceived: just as Jesus was sorrowfully to look at Jerusalem and say, "Would that even today you knew the things that make for peace! But now they are hid from your eyes" (Luke 19:42).

But how do we explain the conflicting views of deeply sincere people all claiming to know God's will? Verse 10 claims that the priests and prophets who opposed Jeremiah had been deliberately used by God to deceive the people. You will find a similar explanation for false prophets in the famous story of the clash between Micaiah and the four hundred prophets in 1 Kings chapter 22. Jeremiah may well have known that story. Yet it is an explanation which does not seem ultimately to have satisfied Jeremiah. It raises awkward questions about the character of God. What kind of God is this who goes round deliberately deceiving people; could we ever completely trust him? We shall find another suggestion in 23:9ff.

Before we stand in judgement on those who did not understand what Jeremiah was saying, let us remember that had we been in Jerusalem in Jeremiah's day we would most likely have been saying "all is well"—and giving the best of religious reasons for so saying. Perhaps we are still saying it too easily today.

THE SEARING WIND OF JUDGEMENT

Jeremiah 4:11–18

11At that time it will be said to this people and to Jerusalem, "A hot wind from the bare heights in the desert toward the daughter of my people, not to winnow or cleanse, 12a wind too full for this comes for me. Now it is I who speak in judgment upon them."

13Behold, he comes up like clouds,
      his chariots like the whirlwind;
   his horses are swifter than eagles—
      woe to us, for we are ruined!
14O Jerusalem, wash your heart from wickedness,
      that you may be saved.
   How long shall your evil thoughts
      lodge within you?
15For a voice declares from Dan
      and proclaims evil from Mount Ephraim.
16Warn the nations that he is coming;
      announce to Jerusalem,
   "Besiegers come from a distant land;
      they shout against the cities of Judah.
17Like keepers of a field are they against her round about,
      because she has rebelled against me,
                              says the Lord.
18Your ways and your doings
      have brought this upon you.
   This is your doom, and it is bitter;
      it has reached your very heart."

The net is closing. From the northern frontier town of Dan near the source of the river Jordan, down through the central highlands of Ephraim not many miles north of Jerusalem, on to the capital itself, the message is carried—the invading hordes are coming. This is God's judgement, vividly compared in verses 11–12 to the sirocco, the hot, dry wind that blows in from the eastern desert, sending the temperature soaring, a menace to the farmer, too violent to be used to separate the chaff from the grain. That it is God's judgement against his own people is underlined by the description of the nation as "the daughter of my people" (verse 11; cf. 8:19, 21, 22) or perhaps more accurately "my daughter-people". It is a term of endearment, stressing God's relationship with, and his care for, Israel. And it is precisely because he does care that he must judge. This is a rebellious daughter. In verse 14 the theme of chapter 3 is heard again; an appeal to the nation to purify its life as the only possible basis for future hope. This is the only time such a note is heard in chapters 4–6; it sounds like a last despairing cry caught up and drowned in the violent storm of inescapable doom.

THE PROPHET'S AGONY

Jeremiah 4:19–28

19My anguish, my anguish! I writhe in pain!
 Oh, the walls of my heart!
My heart is beating wildly;
 I cannot keep silent;
for I hear the sound of the trumpet,
 the alarm of war.
20Disaster follows hard on disaster,
 the whole land is laid waste.
Suddenly my tents are destroyed,
 my curtains in a moment.
21How long must I see the standard,
 and hear the sound of the trumpet?
22"For my people are foolish,
 they know me not;
they are stupid children,
 they have no understanding.
They are skilled in doing evil,
 but how to do good they know not."

23I looked on the earth, and lo, it was waste and void;
 and to the heavens, and they had no light.
24I looked on the mountains, and lo, they were quaking,
 and all the hills moved to and fro.
25I looked, and lo, there was no man,
 and all the birds of the air had fled.

²⁶I looked, and lo, the fruitful land was a desert,
  and all its cities were laid in ruins
  before the Lord, before his fierce anger.
²⁷For thus says the Lord, "The whole land shall be a desolation; yet I
  will not make a full end.
²⁸For this the earth shall mourn,
  and the heavens above be black;
for I have spoken, I have purposed;
  I have not relented nor will I turn back."

Disaster upon disaster—this is God's message; it must be spoken, but Jeremiah cannot proclaim it with calm indifference or studied self-control. He is God's messenger, but he is also one of the people. He cannot help but identify with them in their tragedy. There can be for him no personal haven of spiritual calm, while his people perish (cf. 8:18–19). As the fabric of the nation's life collapses, so does the fabric of his inner life collapse like a tent suddenly destroyed. He bursts out:

My anguish, my anguish! I writhe in pain!

More literally the Hebrew could be rendered "O my bowels, my bowels! I writhe!" The Hebrews located different psychological experiences in different parts of the body. The bowels were regarded as the seat of powerful emotions; see Isa. 16:11 where the Hebrew which would literally be rendered "my bowels rumble" is rightly translated by the NEB as "my heart throbs". So in Col. 3:12 where "bowels of mercy" (AV) is rightly translated in most modern versions as "compassion".

The cost of being a prophet for Jeremiah is not merely the cost of preaching an unpopular message to which few paid any attention; it involves inner turmoil, surging emotions which threaten to tear him apart. He is being pushed to the point when he feels he can no longer stand the strain. He is haunted by the same agonised question that puzzled Job and many of the Psalmists (see Ps. 13:1–2; Ps. 74:1; Job 24:1)—how long? Into his perplexity there comes a word from the Lord (verse 22), not a reassuring word, but a word that affirms that there is no alternative to national tragedy. The people are clueless as to how truly to respond to God. The only skill they possess is the skill to do evil.

In verses 23–26 we find one of the most striking and dramatic prophetic visions in the Old Testament. Four times we listen to the echoing "I looked...", and what the prophet saw was the world he knew dissolving into the unordered, primeval chaos out of which at the beginning God had created the world. Read Genesis chapter 1, for this is the story of Genesis chapter 1 in reverse. It is like a film being run backwards:

—the earth returning to "waste and void", that formless, shapeless chaos out of which it had come (Gen. 1:2)

—light being replaced again by darkness (Gen. 1:3)

—the mountains and the hills, symbols of stability and of God's right ordering of the world (see Ps. 36:6), quaking and shaking

—a world uninhabited, no man (contrast Gen. 1:26f.), no birds (contrast Gen. 1:22)

—a fertile world returning to a plantless desert (contrast Gen. 1:11ff.), ruined cities.

All that makes life possible and meaningful in a God-ordered world gone. The Old Testament does not think of man apart from the world in which he lives. The chaos in society is reflected in the chaos in that wider world. And we are being forced again today to take with ever greater seriousness the fact that for good and for ill our lives are bound up with our natural environment. We can destroy both it and ourselves.

The vision is confirmed by another word from the Lord; a universe plunged into mourning, that is God's intention and from it he will not turn. Unless verse 27 is to be taken as the comment of a later writer attempting to insert a ray of hope into Jeremiah's sombre picture of total destruction, it is better translated without the negative:

The whole land shall be a desolation,
I will surely make a complete end of it.

The prophets whose message was of lasting value never trifle with evil. They never say it does not matter. They believe that God takes it with deadly seriousness.

A COMMUNITY WITHOUT EXCUSE

Jeremiah 4:29–5:9

29 At the noise of horseman and archer
   every city takes to flight;
  they enter thickets; they climb among rocks;
   all the cities are forsaken,
   and no man dwells in them.
30 And you, O desolate one,
  what do you mean that you dress in scarlet,
   that you deck yourself with ornaments of gold,
   that you enlarge your eyes with paint?
  In vain you beautify yourself.
   Your lovers despise you;
   they seek your life.
31 For I heard a cry as of a woman in travail,
   anguish as of one bringing forth her first child,
  the cry of the daughter of Zion gasping for breath,
   stretching out her hands,
  "Woe is me! I am fainting before murderers."

1 Run to and fro through the streets of Jerusalem,
   look and take note!
  Search her squares to see
   if you can find a man,
  one who does justice
   and seeks truth;
   that I may pardon her.
2 Though they say, "As the Lord lives,"
   yet they swear falsely.
3 O Lord, do not thy eyes look for truth?
  Thou hast smitten them,
   but they felt no anguish;
  thou hast consumed them,
   but they refused to take correction.
  They have made their faces harder than rock;
   they have refused to repent.

4 Then I said, "These are only the poor,
   they have no sense;
  for they do not know the way of the Lord,

the law of their God.
⁵I will go to the great,
    and will speak to them;
for they know the way of the Lord,
    the law of their God."
But they all alike had broken the yoke,
    they had burst the bonds.

⁶Therefore a lion from the forest shall slay them,
    a wolf from the desert shall destroy them.
A leopard is watching against their cities,
    every one who goes out of them shall be torn in pieces;
because their transgressions are many,
    their apostasies are great.

⁷"How can I pardon you?
    Your children have forsaken me,
    and have sworn by those who are no gods.
When I fed them to the full,
    they committed adultery
    and trooped to the houses of harlots.
⁸They were well-fed lusty stallions,
    each neighing for his neighbour's wife.
⁹Shall I not punish them for these things?
                                    says the Lord;
    and shall I not avenge myself
    on a nation such as this?"

The final words on national collapse in chapter 4 return to the
picture of Israel the prostitute. We see her decking herself up to
the nines, carefully applying her eye-shadow—enlarged eyes
being a sign of beauty in the ancient world—titivating herself for
what she believes to be an assignation with her lovers. Little does
she know she is making an appointment with death. The picture
of this pleasure-seeking prostitute fades into that of a woman in
labour with her first child, screaming with pain, gasping for
breath, her hands clenched. Israel is paying the price for her
promiscuous conduct. Her lovers have turned out to be her
murderers.

Any lingering doubts about the rightness of the death sentence
God has passed on the people are dispelled in the ensuing dia-

logue (5:1–9) between the Lord and Jeremiah. It begins, verses 1–2, with the Lord issuing a challenge to Jeremiah. There are plenty people in Jerusalem who make a false profession of faith; produce one man who genuinely expresses that right living which is the only response in which the Lord is interested. Produce one such man, says the Lord, and I will forgive the city. Do you remember the story in Gen. 18:22–33 in which Abraham prays to the Lord on behalf of the city of Sodom? Eventually Abraham persuades the Lord to forgive Sodom if only ten righteous men can be found in the city. It is as if God is now saying to Jeremiah: "It seems to me that Jerusalem is worse than pagan Sodom; prove me wrong, if you can, by producing just one righteous man".

Jeremiah responds to the challenge in verses 3–6, but has to admit defeat. From bitter past experience the people have learned nothing. They stubbornly refuse to repent (turn). Some of them, claims Jeremiah, have an excuse. They can hardly be expected to know any better. He describes them as "the poor" or "the weak" (verse 4). This does not necessarily refer to people below the subsistence level economically. It probably means here no more than ordinary folk who do not normally think for themselves or make any claims to be deeply religious. They are decent folk if properly led; and it is to the leadership in the community, "the great", that Jeremiah turns. They ought to have known what was expected of them in the light of God's revelation of himself. Perhaps they do know, but they are no more responsive to the Lord than a runaway ox is to its owner. Such a straying animal is an obvious meal for marauding predators, lion, wolf or prowling leopard; so the people having strayed from the Lord may expect to be torn to pieces.

The Lord's reply in verses 7–9 begins with a question and ends with a question, the first question virtually saying "diagnosis correct, how can I forgive?" The final question dares anyone to dispute this decision. In between there is a catalogue of some of the sins of the community:

(i) religious apostasy, pathetic in its futility, since it means worshipping gods who are "no gods" (verse 7*a*);

(ii) social corruption exemplified in prostitution and adultery (verses 7*b*, 8).

Perhaps these particular social evils are picked out because of their obvious relationship with the sexual element in the worship of the fertility gods and goddesses. It is hardly surprising that what religion encouraged was regarded as socially acceptable. What, and how, a community worships inevitably influences its sense of values.

A FAITHLESS COMMUNITY UNDER JUDGEMENT (i)

Jeremiah 5:10–31

> [10]"Go up through her vine-rows and destroy,
>   but make not a full end;
>   strip away her branches,
>   for they are not the Lord's.
> [11]For the house of Israel and the house of Judah
>   have been utterly faithless to me,
>   says the Lord.
> [12]They have spoken falsely of the Lord,
>   and have said, 'He will do nothing;
>   no evil will come upon us,
>   nor shall we see sword or famine.
> [13]The prophets will become wind;
>   the word is not in them.
>   Thus shall it be done to them!'"
>
> [14]Therefore thus says the Lord, the God of hosts:
>   "Because they have spoken this word,
>   behold, I am making my words in your mouth a fire,
>   and this people wood, and the fire shall devour them.
> [15]Behold, I am bringing upon you
>   a nation from afar, O house of Israel,
>   says the Lord.
>   It is an enduring nation,
>   it is an ancient nation,
>   a nation whose language you do not know,
>   nor can you understand what they say.
> [16]Their quiver is like an open tomb,
>   they are all mighty men.
> [17]They shall eat up your harvest and your food;

> they shall eat up your sons and your daughters;
> they shall eat up your flocks and your herds;
>> they shall eat up your vines and your fig trees;
> your fortified cities in which you trust
>> they shall destroy with the sword."

18"But even in those days, says the Lord, I will not make a full end of you. 19And when your people say, 'Why has the Lord our God done all these things to us?' you shall say to them, 'As you have forsaken me and served foreign gods in your land, so you shall serve strangers in a land that is not yours.'"

20Declare this in the house of Jacob,
>> proclaim it in Judah:
21"Hear this, O foolish and senseless people,
>> who have eyes, but see not,
>> who have ears, but hear not.
22Do you not fear me? says the Lord;
>> Do you not tremble before me?
> I placed the sand as the bound for the sea,
>> a perpetual barrier which it cannot pass;
> though the waves toss, they cannot prevail,
>> though they roar, they cannot pass over it.
23But this people has a stubborn and rebellious heart;
>> they have turned aside and gone away.
24They do not say in their hearts,
>> 'Let us fear the Lord our God,
> who gives the rain in its season,
>> the autumn rain and the spring rain,
> and keeps for us
>> the weeks appointed for the harvest.'
25Your iniquities have turned these away,
>> and your sins have kept good from you.
26For wicked men are found among my people;
>> they lurk like fowlers lying in wait.
> They set a trap;
>> they catch men.
27Like a basket full of birds,
>> their houses are full of treachery;
> therefore they have become great and rich,
28   they have grown fat and sleek.

They know no bounds in deeds of wickedness;
    they judge not with justice
the cause of the fatherless, to make it prosper,
    and they do not defend the rights of the needy.
29Shall I not punish them for these things?
                        says the Lord,
    and shall I not avenge myself
    on a nation such as this?"

30An appalling and horrible thing
    has happened in the land:
31the prophets prophesy falsely,
    and the priests rule at their direction;
my people love to have it so,
    but what will you do when the end comes?

This long section gathers together a series of brief sermons illustrating some of the basic themes in Jeremiah's teaching. Although one section (verses 15–17) contains a further graphic description of the invader from the north—a powerful, ancient people, speaking a strange foreign lingo—the main interest is not in the agent but in the fact of the Lord's judgement, and the reasons for it.

A FAITHLESS COMMUNITY UNDER JUDGEMENT (ii)

Jeremiah 5:10–31 (*cont'd*)

Let us examine these reasons in more detail.

(1) Here is a community which dismissed God as irrelevant to its life. People say "He will do nothing" (verse 12), literally "not he". This is not intellectual atheism; it is something much more common both in ancient Israel and today, believing in theory that there is a God, but ushering him politely to the touchlines of the universe where he sits, no doubt interested in what is going on, but never doing anything. Around the same time as Jeremiah, the prophet Zephaniah was witnessing exactly the same mood in Jerusalem, with people saying:

The Lord will not do good,
    neither will he do ill. (Zeph. 1:12)

In one way that is a handy god to have; at least he will never interfere in the way you want to live your life. The snag, of course, is that he is not much help when we are in need of it.

(2) Here is a community blind to the real issues of life, people

who have eyes, but see not,
who have ears, but hear not. (verse 21)

Compare Isa. 6:9–10; Matt. 13:14–15. They are blind in particular to the need for that reverent acknowledgement of the claim that God makes upon their lives, what the Old Testament calls "the fear of the Lord" (see verses 22–24). Such an acknowledgement means accepting that we cannot go it alone in life, or merely do our own thing. It is strange, says Jeremiah, how the natural world illustrates the need for boundaries, the sand separating the sea in all its fury from the land (verse 22), and bears constant witness to the goodness and bounty of God. Yet God's people refuse to accept any boundaries; they openly rebel against a bountiful Lord. This strange fact he traces to something that never ceases to fascinate him, that "stubborn and rebellious heart" (verse 23) or, as we might put it, the sheer cussedness in human nature.

(3) Such cussedness can express itself in many ways. Here Jeremiah draws attention to the fact that the wicked and the unscrupulous in society seem to prosper. Like a birdcatcher with a cage full of birds, so the wicked catch people and fill their homes with ill-gotten gains (verses 26–27). Money talks. The law can be manipulated to the detriment of those at risk in society, the poor, the orphans. The "haves" get richer and the "have nots" go from bad to worse. For most of us in the western world the illustration Jeremiah uses of the birdcatcher is not part of our experience, but do we need to look far to find uncomfortable parallels to the point he is making?

(4) The religious leadership of the community again comes under attack, particularly the prophets:

The prophets will become wind;
the word is not in them. (verse 13)

There is biting irony in these words because the Hebrew word translated "wind" may also be translated "spirit". These prophets no doubt claimed to be inspired by the spirit of the Lord: not so, says Jeremiah, they are mere windbags. In verses 30–31 Jeremiah reacts in horrified amazement to the fact that the prophets speak a false, misleading word, and that the priests, who ought to have exercised an all-important teaching ministry, are hand in glove with them in an unholy alliance. Not that the people complain; they are getting the kind of reassuring, undemanding religious leadership that they want. Why go to church to be made to feel uncomfortable?

In this situation the true prophetic word can only be a word of judgement, of fire consuming this rebellious people (verses 14–15). In two verses we hear again the words we discussed at 4:27 "make—or make not—a full end" (verses 10 and 18). The first uses the familiar picture of Israel the vineyard or the vine (see Isa. 5:1–7; Hos. 10:1); there must be a drastic pruning, a stripping away of the branches, "for they are not the Lord's" (verse 10). The other depicts the people, exiled to a foreign land, plaintively asking why such a fate has befallen them, and being told in no uncertain terms that it is because they have forsaken the Lord (verses 18–19).

Both of these pictures could be taken in different ways. The drastic pruning, the exile, could mean that the final curtain has come down on the life of the nation. In this case we should translate "make a full end". Yet the drastic pruning leaves the vine intact and leads to new growth; compare the use which Jesus makes of this homely illustration in John 15:1–2. In exile there survives a remnant of the nation upon which the future may be built. So we may translate "make not a full end" and keep open, even in the midst of catastrophe, a door of hope. Certainly elsewhere there is to be found in the book of Jeremiah just such a passage of hope (see especially chapters 30–33). It is an essential part of the biblical message. The cross would be unrelieved gloom, the darkest of tragedies, if we did not see it through the light of the resurrection.

JERUSALEM UNDER SIEGE—A FINAL WARNING

Jeremiah 6:1–8

> ¹Flee for safety, O people of Benjamin,
>> from the midst of Jerusalem!
> Blow the trumpet in Tekoa,
>> and raise a signal on Beth-hac-cherem;
> for evil looms out of the north,
>> and great destruction.
> ²The comely and delicately bred I will destroy,
>> the daughter of Zion.
> ³Shepherds with their flocks shall come against her;
>> they shall pitch their tents around her,
>> they shall pasture, each in his place.
> ⁴"Prepare war against her;
>> up, and let us attack at noon!"
> "Woe to us, for the day declines,
>> for the shadows of evening lengthen!"
> ⁵"Up, and let us attack by night,
>> and destroy her palaces!"
>
> ⁶For thus says the Lord of hosts:
> "Hew down her trees;
>> cast up a siege mound against Jerusalem.
> This is the city which must be punished;
>> there is nothing but oppression within her.
> ⁷As a well keeps its water fresh,
>> so she keeps fresh her wickedness;
> violence and destruction are heard within her;
>> sickness and wounds are ever before me.
> ⁸Be warned, O Jerusalem,
>> lest I be alienated from you;
> lest I make you a desolation,
>> an uninhabited land."

In 4:5–6 the people were warned to flee to safety from the indefensible countryside into the fortified cities, none greater, none more inviting than Jerusalem. Here Jeremiah counsels "the people of Benjamin", his own fellow-tribesmen (1:1), to flee *from* Jerusalem. Instead of offering security it is a death-trap.

Throughout the land the alarm is sounded: in Tekoa, Amos' home town in the hills south-east of Jerusalem, and in Beth-hac-cherem, probably west of Jerusalem though its exact location is uncertain. The second half of verse 1 contains one of these plays on similar sounding words in Hebrew, which it is almost impossible to convey in English. Perhaps we come a little nearer it if we translate:

> In Tekoa take the trumpet,
> signal a signal (i.e. light a beacon) at Beth-hac-cherem.

The siege of Jerusalem is beginning. As shepherds naturally gravitate to a lush meadow, so the shepherd kings (see commentary on 2:1–13 (*cont'd*)) gather round Jerusalem. In their eagerness to press home the attack, they are prepared to continue military operations after nightfall, not normal military tactics in the ancient world. The trees around the city are felled to make ramps for the battering-rams which will breach the city walls. There can be no escape from God in Jerusalem, because Jerusalem richly deserves coming judgement. From a well there comes ever-fresh water, and from Jerusalem, that sick society, ever-fresh evil (verse 7). A final warning is given, a warning which, if ignored, will lead to the Lord becoming "alienated" from his own people. This is Israel's tragedy; a relationship with God which, rooted in God's loving initiative, began so promisingly, is being destroyed till God becomes no more than a stranger to his own people.

FOR WHOM THE BELL TOLLS

Jeremiah 6:9–15

> 9Thus says the Lord of hosts:
> "Glean thoroughly as a vine
>   the remnant of Israel;
> like a grape-gatherer pass your hand again
>   over its branches."
> 10To whom shall I speak and give warning,

> that they may hear?
> Behold, their ears are closed,
>   they cannot listen;
> behold, the word of the Lord is to them an object of scorn,
>   they take no pleasure in it.
> ¹¹Therefore I am full of the wrath of the Lord;
>   I am weary of holding it in.
> "Pour it out upon the children in the street,
>   and upon the gatherings of young men, also;
> both husband and wife shall be taken,
>   the old folk and the very aged.
> ¹²Their houses shall be turned over to others,
>   their fields and wives together;
> for I will stretch out my hand
>   against the inhabitants of the land,"
>   says the Lord.
> ¹³"For from the least to the greatest of them,
>   every one is greedy for unjust gain;
> and from prophet to priest,
>   every one deals falsely.
> ¹⁴They have healed the wound of my people lightly,
>   saying, 'Peace, peace,'
> when there is no peace.
> ¹⁵Were they ashamed when they committed abomination?
>   No, they were not at all ashamed;
>   they did not know how to blush.
> Therefore they shall fall among those who fall;
>   at the time that I punish them, they shall be overthrown,"
>   says the Lord.

Here is another of Jeremiah's conversations with the Lord. The Lord begins the conversation in verse 9, ordering Jeremiah to act like the "gleaner" who, after the grapes have been gathered, works his way through the vineyard stripping off any grapes that have been left by the harvesters. Once the gleaner has done his work there should be nothing left.

Jeremiah's reply in verses 10–11a shows us something of the strain under which he was living. The whole point of a prophet's ministry is to preach that people may listen, heed the warnings given and turn from their evil ways. Well, I have preached, says

Jeremiah, and for all the good it has done I might as well have kept my breath to cool my porridge. No one is listening, "their ears are closed", uncircumcised, says the Hebrew, using a phrase which is found again in Stephen's speech in Acts 7:51, though in the Old Testament the word uncircumcised is more commonly used metaphorically with reference to lips (Exod. 6:12,30) or heart (Jer. 4:4). Not only are they deaf to what God wants to say to them, but they openly laugh at what the prophet is saying—and there is nothing more soul-destroying than trying to tell people something you believe to be of central importance to their lives, only to be met with ridicule. To preach is pointless; but not to preach is tearing me apart, says Jeremiah. I cannot keep this message of the wrath of God bottled up inside me.

Do not try to bottle it up, says the Lord in reply, pour it out (verse 11ff.). There may be an implied rebuke in these words, as if the Lord were saying to Jeremiah: What do you want to be—a successful preacher? Forget it: I am not asking you to be successful, I am asking you to be faithful. Preach, preach to everyone from the toddlers in the street to the old-age pensioners; all will be caught up in the coming disaster:

> for I will stretch out my hand against the inhabitants of the land.
> (verse 12)

This phrase "stretching out the hand" is often used in the Old Testament to mean striking or clobbering someone. Sometimes it points to the destructive anger of God. A series of passages in the book of Isaiah each ends with the refrain:

> For all this his anger has not turned away,
>   and his hand is stretched out still.
> (Isa. 9:12,17,21; 10:4)

The picture that Jeremiah draws of contemporary society in verses 13-15 is grim. Everyone, "from the least to the greatest"— or as we would say, every Tom, Dick and Harry—is involved in the scramble for wealth and influence, and if others get hurt in the process, that's life, isn't it? Those who ought to have known better, the religious establishment, "from prophet to priest" (verse 13), are encouraging a mood which bears no relationship to what is going on in society. "Peace, peace" or "all is well, all is well", Hebrew *shalom*, is their reassuring message.

There is no one English word which can convey the rich meaning of this word *shalom*. It points to that full, wholesome life under God in which the needs and the rights of all will be respected and met, to that kind of world which we long for in our better moments. But to say "shalom" in the Jerusalem of Jeremiah's day was to be like a quack doctor mouthing reassuring words as he superficially treats a deadly wound (cf. 4:9–10). False complacency marketed without even a blush; they <u>have become so accustomed to trafficking in evil that they no longer recognise it as evil</u>. That is one of the insidious things about evil. The first lie may trouble your conscience; the second is a little less painful; and so it goes on until there comes a time when the lie is told without batting an eyelid. Having squared their own conscience such prophets and priests can hardly be expected to guard the conscience of the community for which they are responsible. They are doomed to share the fate of those whom they have blatantly misled.

We will find verses 13–15 repeated in a different context in 8:10*b*–12.

WRONG CHOICES

Jeremiah 6:16–21

¹⁶Thus says the Lord:
"Stand by the roads, and look,
　and ask for the ancient paths,
where the good way is; and walk in it,
　and find rest for your souls.
But they said, 'We will not walk in it.'
¹⁷I set watchmen over you, saying,
　'Give heed to the sound of the trumpet!'
But they said, 'We will not give heed.'
¹⁸Therefore hear, O nations,
　and know, O congregation, what will happen to them.

¹⁹Hear, O earth; behold, I am bringing evil upon this people,
   the fruit of their devices,
because they have not given heed to my words;
   and as for my law, they have rejected it.
²⁰To what purpose does frankincense come to me from Sheba,
   or sweet cane from a distant land?
Your burnt offerings are not acceptable,
   nor your sacrifices pleasing to me.
²¹Therefore thus says the Lord:
'Behold, I will lay before this people
   stumbling blocks against which they shall stumble;
fathers and sons together,
   neighbour and friend shall perish.'"

<u>This passage begins by describing the people as deliberately
rejecting what could have been their salvation.</u> The words would
be sharply relevant in the years immediately following the
national reformation of 621 B.C. when it was becoming clear to
Jeremiah, if to no one else, that this was a reformation which was
failing to live up to expectation. The reformation was based on
the book of Deuteronomy. Again and again Deuteronomy faces
the people with choices, and spells out the consequences of their
choices. So the people are challenged to "stand by the roads"
(verse 16), the crossroads, and there to choose "the ancient
paths". This is not an appeal to go back to "the good old days".
You will find some wise words on the stupidity of harping back to
the good old days in Ecc. 7:10. It is an appeal to what was central
to Israel's faith from the beginning, that relationship with God
which was the foundation of the nation's life and which alone
could bring true security or "rest". That relationship meant paying heed to the Lord's words and his "law" or teaching, Hebrew
torah (verse 19); responding, according to Deuteronomy, in loving obedience to the love of God (Deut. 6:4–9; 7:6–11).

The other voice to which the people ought to have been listening was the voice of "watchmen" (verse 17), the prophets.
Ezekiel in particular speaks of himself as having been sent as a
watchman to warn the people of the life and death consequences
of the choices they make (Ezek. 3:16–21). But the warnings went

unheeded. Not that the people were anything other than religious. They brought God costly and lavish offerings and thought he would be satisfied; offerings garnished with fragrant "frankincense" imported from Sheba in south-west Arabia, and with "sweet cane" or spices, again brought on the camel trains from Arabia (verse 20). The *burnt offerings* of that verse were a type of sacrifice in which the whole animal was offered as a gift to God upon the altar; the *sacrifices* took the form of a shared meal, a kind of communion, in which certain parts of the sacrifice were given to God on the altar and the rest was consumed together by the priests and the worshippers. So the people flocked to worship and in this way believed that they were doing their bit for God. ... and God's verdict was "not acceptable".

This is not a criticism of sacrifice or worship *per se*, it is a question of the meaning of worship. Worship and the sacrificial system were genuine means of grace in ancient Israel, as worship can be today; but they are no substitute for obedience (see 7:22). Worship divorced from a daily life of commitment to God is no more than a meaningless and dangerous charade, no matter how aesthetically pleasing and impressive it may be; for the God who comes to his people in worship is a God who makes inescapable demands upon them. This the prophets from Amos onwards never allowed the people to forget (see Amos 5:21–24; Isa. 1:12–17). A well-filled church can be spiritually meaningless.

With this passage in mind it is worth turning for a moment to Deuteronomy to listen to some words addressed to Israel near the end of the book: "I call heaven and earth to witness against you this day, that I have set before you life and death, blessing and curse; therefore choose life that you and your descendants may live, loving the Lord your God, obeying his voice, and cleaving to him..." (Deut. 30:19–20). It is Jeremiah's complaint that the people have chosen death. But ironically he summons as his witnesses not heaven and earth, but the *nations* (verse 18), the other peoples among whom Israel lived, as if to say that even these nations, pagans in Israel's eyes, would recognise that God's drastic dealings with his people were justified.

THE ROLE OF THE PROPHET

Jeremiah 6:22–30

²²Thus says the Lord:
"Behold, a people is coming from the north country,
a great nation is stirring from the farthest parts of the earth.
²³They lay hold on bow and spear,
they are cruel and have no mercy,
the sound of them is like the roaring sea;
they ride upon horses,
set in array as a man for battle,
against you, O daughter of Zion!"
²⁴We have heard the report of it,
our hands fall helpless;
anguish has taken hold of us,
pain as of a woman in travail.
²⁵Go not forth into the field,
nor walk on the road;
for the enemy has a sword,
terror is on every side.
²⁶O daughter of my people, gird on sackcloth,
and roll in ashes;
make mourning as for an only son,
most bitter lamentation;
for suddenly the destroyer
will come upon us.

²⁷"I have made you an assayer and tester among my people,
that you may know and assay their ways.
²⁸They are all stubbornly rebellious,
going about with slanders;
they are bronze and iron,
all of them act corruptly.
²⁹The bellows blow fiercely,
the lead is consumed by the fire;
in vain the refining goes on,
for the wicked are not removed.
³⁰Refuse silver they are called,
for the Lord has rejected them."

Verses 22–26 contain a further graphic description of the agent of God's judgement, the foe from the north. In face of this pitiless enemy, whose patrols stalk the countryside, the people are as helpless in their agony as a woman in childbirth. There is *terror on every side* (verse 25), a favourite expression of Jeremiah's. He uses it as a nickname for Pashhur, the priest in charge of the Temple, who tries to silence him by putting him in the stocks (20:3): he imagines he hears it applied to himself in the whispering campaign which seeks to discredit him as a prophet (20:10). All that is left is for the people to go into mourning, bitter mourning like the mourning at the death of an only son (verse 26). The death of an only son meant the end of the family, since only he could carry the family name to the next generation. There could be no more tragic experience. Amos 8:10 uses the same illustration in speaking about the day of God's judgement.

And what in all this is the role of the prophet? He is to act as an *assayer* (verse 27), a refiner who tests the purity of precious metal. In the refining process silver ore is placed in a crucible along with lead. Heated to a certain temperature the lead oxidises and carries off any alloy impurities from the silver. Try to refine my people, says the Lord to Jeremiah, and you will find it an impossible task. They are corrupt through and through, as impure as reject silver or dross, fit for nothing but to be thrown on the slag heap.

But how long would a refiner continue in business if all he ever got was dross? "Corrupt through and through"—is this all that Jeremiah has to say about his people? If so, is his ministry not an exercise in futility? This was a question which was to haunt Jeremiah.

C. FALSE RELIGION (7:1–8:3)

AN UNPOPULAR SERMON (i)

Jeremiah 7:1–15

¹The word that came to Jeremiah from the Lord: ²"Stand in the gate of

the Lord's house, and proclaim there this word, and say, Hear the word of the Lord, all you men of Judah who enter these gates to worship the Lord. ³Thus says the Lord of hosts, the God of Israel, Amend your ways and your doings, and I will let you dwell in this place. ⁴Do not trust in these deceptive words: 'This is the temple of the Lord, the temple of the Lord, the temple of the Lord.'

⁵"For if you truly amend your ways and your doings, if you truly execute justice one with another, ⁶if you do not oppress the alien, the fatherless or the widow, or shed innocent blood in this place, and if you do not go after other gods to your own hurt, ⁷then I will let you dwell in this place, in the land that I gave of old to your fathers for ever.

⁸"Behold, you trust in deceptive words to no avail. ⁹Will you steal, murder, commit adultery, swear falsely, burn incense to Baal, and go after other gods that you have not known, ¹⁰and then come and stand before me in this house, which is called by my name, and say, 'We are delivered!'—only to go on doing all these abominations? ¹¹Has this house, which is called by my name, become a den of robbers in your eyes? Behold, I myself have seen it, says the Lord. ¹²Go now to my place that was in Shiloh, where I made my name dwell at first, and see what I did to it for the wickedness of my people Israel. ¹³And now, because you have done all these things, says the Lord, and when I spoke to you persistently you did not listen, and when I called you, you did not answer, ¹⁴therefore I will do to the house which is called by my name, and in which you trust, and to the place which I gave to you and to your fathers, as I did to Shiloh. ¹⁵And I will cast you out of my sight, as I cast out all your kinsmen, all the offspring of Ephraim."

A glance at any modern English translation will immediately show you that from the beginning of chapter 7 to chapter 8:3 we have the first long prose section in the book of Jeremiah. Such prose narratives—and there are many of them in the book of Jeremiah (see 11:1–17; 13:1–14; 16:1–18; 18:1–12; 19:1–20:6)— often centre upon an incident in Jeremiah's life, and related to the incident a sermon. Who wrote these accounts and sermons we do not know, though some of them may be the work of Jeremiah's friend and secretary Baruch (see 32:12ff.; 36:14ff.). To what extent they take us back to the actual words Jeremiah used on such occasions it is impossible to say since the reports have been written up by later editors, and their interests, outlook and prejudices have coloured the presentation. Think of the way in which even today the same incident, for example a protest gathering in the streets of Warsaw, is differently presented by Polish State Television, the BBC and NBC. If that happens in what is virtually on the spot reporting, how much more will it affect reports written years after the events.

There is little doubt, however, that these passages spring from genuine incidents in the life and ministry of Jeremiah, and of this the Temple Sermon in 7:1–15 is an excellent example. Towards the end of chapter 6 we heard three themes:

   (i) the futility of much that passes for worship in the community (6:20–21)
  (ii) coming disaster and the destruction of the community (6:22–24)
 (iii) the prophet's role as the refiner or tester of the people (6:27–30).

These three themes are now illustrated in the narrative in 7:1–8:3, in which we find a number of scathing attacks on the false religious practices of the people.

Turn to chapter 26 where you will find another account of Jeremiah's unpopular sermon. Chapter 26 says little about the content of the sermon. It concentrates instead on the audience reaction, and in particular on the way in which different sections in the community reacted differently—the religious establishment (priests and prophets) demanding the death penalty, the civil authorities (the princes) acquitting the prophet of the charge of treason, and the ordinary people, as not uncommonly, apparently changing their minds (compare 26:7 with 26:16). All of which suggests that this was no run of the mill sermon; it got under people's skin. It was sharp enough to offend, to divide the community, and to make people think.

Chapter 26:1 gives the date of the sermon, "the beginning of the reign of Jehoiakim the son of Josiah, king of Judah"; it was delivered, therefore, sometime in the autumn of 609 B.C. or the winter of 609/608 B.C. The date is significant. Josiah, the reforming king, on whom great hopes for national renewal had been pinned, was dead, killed at the battle of Megiddo, fighting for his nation's independence (2 Kings 23:28–30). Jehoiakim was king by grace of his Egyptian overlord. The first shock had been administered to the resurgent Judean religious nationalism for which Josiah stood.

But it had one trump card left—Jerusalem and its Temple (see comment on 4:10). Here is where the Lord dwells in the midst of his people:

> This is my resting place for ever;
> here I will dwell, for I have desired it. (Ps. 132:14)

Because this was "the temple of the Lord" (verse 4) all would and must be well with Jerusalem. It is this deep belief that Jeremiah attacks in his sermon, delivered probably at the entrance to the inner court of the Temple as the people gathered for worship on some great national religious festival.

AN UNPOPULAR SERMON (ii)

Jeremiah 7:1–15 (*cont'd*)

Jeremiah's sermon is noteworthy for several reasons:

(1) He addresses the worshippers in the name of "the Lord of hosts, the God of Israel" (verse 3), the God whose presence and protecting power they came to celebrate in worship. Now Jeremiah is not denying that God is present with his people; but he is warning them not to draw the wrong conclusion from this. God's presence can be a dangerous presence to those who trifle with him (see the comment on 2:19).

(2) The sermon is at heart a call for a radical change of life-style: "Amend your ways and your doings" (verse 3). And it spells this out in a series of "ifs" (verses 5–6). The kind of life-style God expects from his people means unquestioning loyalty to the one God, a loyalty which will find practical expression in a caring society. Only if that call is heeded can the people lay

claim—as they are only too anxious to do—to the promises of God: "then I will let you dwell in this place" (verses 3,7) or perhaps better, with some versions of the text, "then I will dwell with you in this place".

It is best to take the word "place" throughout the sermon to refer to the Temple, the holy place, rather than to the city. The preacher's call is urgent since everything points to the conduct of the worshippers giving the lie to what they profess in worship. They claim to be God's people yet verses 8–10 provide us with a sorry catalogue of violations of most of the Ten Commandments. So when they come to the Temple, chant "this is the temple of the Lord, the temple of the Lord, the temple of the Lord" (verse 4), and then claim "we are delivered" (verse 10), they are living in a fool's paradise, trusting in words which are no better than a lie. With biting irony Jeremiah protests that this is to treat the Temple as if it were a bandits' hideaway, a "den of robbers" (verse 11), to which those who are on the run from the law of God retreat. Jesus, according to Mark 11:17, in an equally scathing attack on what was going on in the Temple in his day, uses these words, contrasting them with the true picture in Isaiah chapter 56 of the Temple as "a house of prayer for all nations".

(3) If the call goes unheeded—and the people's past record is anything but reassuring (verse 13)—then, says Jeremiah, the Temple, far from being a place of safety, will be turned into a desolate site. This is a direct attack on the mood in Jerusalem which was saying, "It can't happen to us". Learn the lesson of Shiloh, says Jeremiah. Shiloh, in the highlands of Ephraim, had once been a very important centre for the worship of the Lord of hosts, as can be seen in the stories in 1 Samuel chapters 1–4. The temple at Shiloh had once housed the ark, the sacred symbol of God's presence in the midst of his people (see comment on 3:16). But in Jeremiah's day it was a ruin, devastated by the Philistines in the eleventh century B.C. and probably finally destroyed by the Assyrians towards the end of the eighth century. Of course Shiloh was in the north, and people in Jerusalem were liable to say that these pagan northerners had just got what they deserved. And so will you, says Jeremiah. There will come a day when the Jeru-

salem Temple will become like the temple at Shiloh, and you, like the northerners you despise, will go off into exile (verse 15).

This is not popular preaching. It is too near the bone for that. People do not like to have their deeply ingrained prejudices called into question—particularly if they are religious prejudices. Worship is there to comfort, not to upset. There are two things, however, about this unpopular sermon worth pondering.

(1) Much of what Jeremiah is here saying is not new. That worship divorced from daily living is a dangerous self-deception was something that worship itself ought to have taught those who flocked to the Temple. Look at some of the Psalms, in particular Psalms 15 and 24:3–6. They were almost certainly used in antiphonal singing in the Temple. The worshipper asks the question:

O Lord, who shall sojourn in thy tent?
 who shall dwell on thy holy hill? (Ps. 15:1)

and receives from the priest an answer that challenges him to look at the way he lives (Ps. 15:2–5)—do what is right, speak the truth, don't cheat your neighbour, don't take bribes. The trouble of course is that we often hear only what we want to hear, and to the rest we turn a deaf ear. Nowhere is this more true than in worship.

(2) Faith is based on God's promises, but we dare not convert these promises into unconditional certainties. The promises made to Abraham, for example, in Gen. 12:2–3 could only come true if he were prepared to leave his family home and go out into the unknown. No human relationship can deepen if it is only one sided; no more can our relationship with God. To ignore the continuing "if" in faith is to court disaster. When worship and faith seem to lose their meaning for us, it is wise to begin by taking a close look at our own life-style and ask whether we have been living in the light of the demands that faith makes upon us.

THE TIME FOR PRAYER IS OVER

Jeremiah 7:16–20

16"As for you, do not pray for this people, or lift up cry or prayer for them, and do not intercede with me, for I do not hear you. ¹⁷Do you not see what they are doing in the cities of Judah and in the streets of Jerusalem? ¹⁸The children gather wood, the fathers kindle fire, and the women knead dough, to make cakes for the queen of heaven; and they pour out drink offerings to other gods, to provoke me to anger. ¹⁹Is it I whom they provoke? says the Lord. Is it not themselves, to their own confusion? ²⁰Therefore thus says the Lord God: Behold, my anger and my wrath will be poured out on this place, upon man and beast, upon the trees of the field and the fruit of the ground; it will burn and not be quenched."

Unlike the sermon in verses 1–15 in which Jeremiah is speaking to the people, in this passage the Lord is speaking to Jeremiah. He begins with what may seem at first a strange order, "do not pray for this people" (verse 16), words that we find repeated in 11:14 and 14:11. We tend to think of a prophet as being on God's side, God's messenger to the people, but a prophet—and none more so than Jeremiah—also represented the people before God. It was one of his privileges to pray on behalf of the people (see, for example 15:11). But the time for praying on behalf of the people is now over. There is no sign that they are at all interested in changing their attitude, steeped as they are in religious practices which, although they do not seem to know it, can only hurt themselves (verse 19).

The worship of the "queen of heaven" (verse 18) seems to have been particularly popular among the women in Judah. It survived the destruction of Jerusalem and flourished among the Jews exiled in Egypt, according to 44:15ff. Who this "queen of heaven" was is not entirely clear, though she was probably one form of a mother fertility goddess known to us from Assyrian, Babylonian and Canaanite sources. Her worship was popular because she was a woman's goddess, appealing to certain basic human instincts, in particular sexuality, motherhood and the desire to know what the future holds in store; just the things that are catered for today in women's magazines and the horoscopes in the daily papers. Perhaps many people thought the worship of the Lord in the Jerusalem Temple was too austere, too remote from their everyday needs. The worship of this goddess seems to have been simple and homely; a little incense, the offering of a libation of wine or of cakes stamped with the image of the goddess or shaped like a crescent moon or a star. Harmless? No, fatal . . . part of that confused set of values that leads to inevitable disaster.

A PEOPLE BLIND TO ESSENTIALS

Jeremiah 7:21–28

21Thus says the Lord of hosts, the God of Israel: "Add your burnt offerings to your sacrifices, and eat the flesh. 22For in the day that I brought them out of the land of Egypt, I did not speak to your fathers or command them concerning burnt offerings and sacrifices. 23But this command I gave them, 'Obey my voice, and I will be your God, and you shall be my people; and walk in all the way that I command you, that it may be well with you.' 24But they did not obey or incline their ear, but walked in their own counsels and the stubbornness of their evil hearts, and went backward and not forward. 25From the day that your fathers came out of the land of Egypt to this day, I have persistently sent all my servants the prophets to them, day after day; 26yet they did not listen to me, or incline their ear, but stiffened their neck. They did worse than their fathers.

27"So you shall speak all these words to them, but they will not listen to you. You shall call to them, but they will not answer you. 28And you shall say to them, 'This is the nation that did not obey the voice of the Lord their God, and did not accept discipline; truth has perished; it is cut off from their lips.'"

In verses 21–28 we find perhaps the most extreme statement of an attitude to the offering of sacrifices which is common in prophetic teaching—see Amos 5:21–24; Mic. 6:6–8; Isa. 1:10–17—and which we have already noted in our comments on 6:20. This passage takes us back to the Exodus, to the story of the beginning of that relationship between the Lord and Israel, which we describe in the word *covenant*, a relationship summed up in the words "I will be your God, and you shall be my people" (verse 23). Nothing was said, claims this passage, about burnt offerings or sacrifices when God established this relationship. Instead there was the demand for obedience, an obedience which has been singularly lacking throughout Israel's history, in spite of God's repeated attempts through "his servants the prophets" to remind the people of their obligations (verses 24–26).

In fact if you look back to the story of covenant in the book of Exodus, you will see that burnt offerings and sacrifices are mentioned (Exod. 24:5); but it is interesting that the Ten Commandments (Exod. 20:1–17), which we may regard as the basic charter of the covenant, have nothing to say about sacrifice. What Jeremiah is claiming here is that as far as Israel is concerned the only indispensable element in her relationship with God is a response of obedience to the ethical and social demands God makes upon his people. This is not to say that sacrifice is not *important* to Israel's faith. It could be a means of grace. But sacrifice is not *essential* to Israel's faith. It could find expression in other ways of worship, as it had to during the Exile in Babylon where there was no possibility of offering sacrifice, and as it has had to in the Jewish community for the last 1,900 years. Take away, however, obedience to the commandments of God which are there to shape daily life, and nothing is left. It is a good thing to be made to think at times about what are the essentials of faith, as opposed to the many things which are no doubt helpful and useful, but which in the end of the day we could do without.

A FATAL DISEASE

Jeremiah 7:29–8:3

29"Cut off your hair and cast it away;
   raise a lamentation on the bare heights,
 for the Lord has rejected and forsaken
   the generation of his wrath.
   30"For the sons of Judah have done evil in my sight, says the Lord; they have set their abominations in the house which is called by my name, to defile it. 31And they have built the high place of Topheth, which is in the valley of the son of Hinnom, to burn their sons and their

daughters in the fire; which I did not command, nor did it come into my mind. [32]Therefore, behold, the days are coming, says the Lord, when it will no more be called Topheth, or the valley of the son of Hinnom, but the valley of Slaughter: for they will bury in Topheth, because there is no room elsewhere. [33]And the dead bodies of this people will be food for the birds of the air, and for the beasts of the earth; and none will frighten them away. [34]And I will make to cease from the cities of Judah and from the streets of Jerusalem the voice of mirth and the voice of gladness, the voice of the bridegroom and the voice of the bride; for the land shall become a waste.

[1]"At that time, says the Lord, the bones of the kings of Judah, the bones of its princes, the bones of the priests, the bones of the prophets, and the bones of the inhabitants of Jerusalem shall be brought out of their tombs; [2]and they shall be spread before the sun and the moon and all the host of heaven, which they have loved and served, which they have gone after, and which they have sought and worshipped; and they shall not be gathered or buried; they shall be as dung on the surface of the ground. [3]Death shall be preferred to life by all the remnant that remains of this evil family in all the places where I have driven them, says the Lord of hosts."

Religion ought to be a thing of joy and gladness, but with bitter irony this picture of religion in Jeremiah's day—the final one in the section on False Religion—is introduced by a "*lament*" or mourning song (Hebrew *qinah*). As we know from other Old Testament passages, for example Job 1:20, cutting off the hair or shaving the head was one of the accepted signs of mourning. And mourning was in order since God had abandoned a community that richly deserved his anger. Instead of bringing health to the community, religion, cancer-like, had proved to be a fatal disease. There was plenty of religion around . . . of a kind:

(1) Symbols and images of other deities called, as not infrequently in the Old Testament, "abominations" (verse 30) were common in the Temple of the Lord on Mount Zion. After all there was no harm in hedging your religious bets, and having as many gods and goddesses as possible on your side.

(2) Child sacrifice was being practised in the valley of Ben Hinnom to the south of Jerusalem, at the high place or shrine of

Topheth (verse 31). The word *Topheth* is related to words meaning "burning", and may signify "fire altars". The narrative in 2 Kings 23:10 says that child sacrifice was offered there to the god Molech, but these verses seem to imply that the worshippers mistakenly thought that this was one of the ways to show their devotion to the Lord. The more costly the gift, the more likely he would be to protect them. They were to be disillusioned. This valley of mistaken religious enthusiasm was to be renamed "the valley of Slaughter", and turned into a gigantic graveyard—the last words of verse 32 should probably be translated "till there is no room left". Indeed it was worse than a graveyard, since in a graveyard bodies are given decent burial. Here devastation is so complete that bodies lie unburied, carrion for birds of prey and scavenging animals. Verses 33–34 describe graphically the silence of death descending upon the land. An appalling practice brings an appalling nemesis.

(3) Astral cults, the worship of the various heavenly bodies, sun, moon and different planets, had wide popular currency among ordinary people in Judah, for the same reason as horoscopes are popular today. Do such heavenly bodies have any influence over people's lives? Not at all, says this passage; they can but look down coldly and silently upon the corpses of their ardent devotees, scattered like "dung on the surface of the ground" (8:2).

The lot of the survivors of the coming holocaust is described as being more tragic than its victims. If this makes grim reading, so be it. Jeremiah never allowed his people the comfort of self-deception. The false had to be destroyed; illusory security had to be shattered. Only then could there be any word of hope.

D. THE END OF THE ROAD (8:4–10:25)

BLIND COMPLACENCY

Jeremiah 8:4–12

4"You shall say to them, Thus says the Lord:
When men fall, do they not rise again?

If one turns away, does he not return?
⁵Why then has this people turned away
　　in perpetual backsliding?
They hold fast to deceit,
　　they refuse to return.
⁶I have given heed and listened,
　　but they have not spoken aright;
no man repents of his wickedness,
　　saying, 'What have I done?'
Every one turns to his own course,
　　like a horse plunging headlong into battle.
⁷Even the stork in the heavens
　　knows her times;
and the turtledove, swallow, and crane
　　keep the time of their coming;
but my people know not
　　the ordinance of the Lord.

⁸"How can you say, 'We are wise,
　　and the law of the Lord is with us'?
But, behold, the false pen of the scribes
　　has made it into a lie.
⁹The wise men shall be put to shame,
　　they shall be dismayed and taken;
lo, they have rejected the word of the Lord,
　　and what wisdom is in them?
¹⁰Therefore I will give their wives to others
　　and their fields to conquerors,
because from the least to the greatest
　　every one is greedy for unjust gain;
from prophet to priest
　　every one deals falsely.
¹¹They have healed the wound of my people lightly,
　　saying, 'Peace, peace,'
　　when there is no peace.
¹²Were they ashamed when they committed abomination?
　　No, they were not at all ashamed;
　　they did not know how to blush.
Therefore they shall fall among the fallen;
　　when I punish them, they shall be overthrown,"
　　　　　　　　　　　　　　　　says the Lord.

From chapter 8:4 to the end of chapter 10 we have a collection of passages, mainly brief and in poetry, very similar in theme to chapters 2–6. But there is one difference. No longer is there—as there was in the middle of these chapters—any call to the people to repent, no longer any expectation that they will. The one passage that plays on the different meanings of the Hebrew word *shuv* (see chapters 3:1–4:3) is the first, and it only serves to underline that repentance is strangely impossible. Much of the material in chapters 8–10 may come from the period when the prophet had become disillusioned with the failure of the reformation of 621 B.C. to affect any radical or lasting change in the life of the people.

Verses 4–7 are introduced as God's word to the people through the prophet, but they could equally well represent Jeremiah's thoughts on what to him was the puzzling, irrational conduct of the people. The natural thing to do when you fall is to pick yourself up. You learn by experience. But apparently God's people do not. This point is hammered home in the second half of verse 4 and in verse 5. Five times forms of the word *shuv*, "turn", are used. We might translate:

> Does one turn (aside) and not turn back?
> Why is this a turncoat people,
> involved in perpetual turning?
> They resort to deceit,
> they refuse to turn.

True they turn, but only to pursue their own wicked schemes, like a horse careering into battle. How strange! Look at the migratory birds; they instinctively know when their time has come to migrate, yet God's people do not seem to know what ought to regulate their lives—the demands God makes upon them. There is some uncertainty about the identification of the birds mentioned in verse 7, particularly the one translated "crane" in the RSV, but there is no uncertainty about the point Jeremiah is making. We tend to think of our failures and our disloyalty to God as being somehow natural—after all we are all sinners, are we not? They are in fact "unnatural", out of character for those who claim to be committed to God. Our homing instinct should be towards God, not away from him.

Verses 8 and 9 raise difficult questions of interpretation. Who are "the scribes"? What is meant by "the law of the Lord"? How was it being falsified or "turned into a lie"? The clue to the meaning of the passage probably lies in the contrast drawn between "the law of the Lord", which the people claim makes them wise, and "the word of the Lord", which they reject.

The "law of the Lord" may well be Deuteronomy or that part of the book which was the basis of the reformation in 621 B.C. Having accepted the book and its teaching the people now claim to be enlightened. Jeremiah does not attack "the law of the Lord", but even the most sacred and authoritative book needs to be interpreted. We must assume, then, that the scribes who were responsible for copying the book, and perhaps expounding it to the people, so interpreted it falsely that the people were prevented from facing the challenge of the living word of the Lord on the lips of the prophet. There is no reason to question the sincerity of these scribes, but they may have been encouraging the people to listen to the promises in the book—and there are many in Deuteronomy—but to forget that such promises were conditional. The written word was fostering a mood of self-complacent optimism against which Jeremiah protests.

Hence the appropriateness in this context of verses 10–12, that passage about "priests and prophets" which we have already studied in 6:13–15. The written word can still kill the living word of God. It is possible to hide from God behind the words "the Bible says". A selection of texts from the Bible can often tell us more about the prejudices of the person who selects them, than about what God is seeking to say to us today.

A PEOPLE IN DESPAIR: A PROPHET IN ANGUISH

Jeremiah 8:13–9:1

13"When I would gather them, says the Lord,
    there are no grapes on the vine,

nor figs on the fig tree;
even the leaves are withered,
    and what I gave them has passed away from them."

¹⁴Why do we sit still?
Gather together, let us go into the fortified cities
    and perish there;
for the Lord our God has doomed us to perish,
    and has given us poisoned water to drink,
    because we have sinned against the Lord.
¹⁵We looked for peace, but no good came,
    for a time of healing, but behold, terror.

¹⁶"The snorting of their horses is heard from Dan;
    at the sound of the neighing of their stallions
    the whole land quakes.
They come and devour the land and all that fills it,
    the city and those who dwell in it.
¹⁷For behold, I am sending among you serpents,
    adders which cannot be charmed,
    and they shall bite you,"
                                    says the Lord.

¹⁸My grief is beyond healing,
    my heart is sick within me.
¹⁹Hark, the cry of the daughter of my people
    from the length and breadth of the land:
"Is the Lord not in Zion?
    Is her King not in her?"
"Why have they provoked me to anger with their graven images,
    and with their foreign idols?"
²⁰"The harvest is past, the summer is ended,
    and we are not saved."
²¹For the wound of the daughter of my people is my heart wounded,
    I mourn, and dismay has taken hold on me.

²²Is there no balm in Gilead?
    Is there no physician there?
Why then has the health of the daughter of my people
    not been restored?
¹O that my head were waters,
    and my eyes a fountain of tears,

that I might weep day and night
for the slain of the daughter of my people!

Verses 13–17 begin and end with a brief word from the Lord, a word of stern judgement. At the beginning the picture of Israel as the vine is used again: but this is a barren vine, a barren fig tree whose very leaves have withered. At the end (verse 17) there is the picture of God letting loose among the people poisonous snakes, snakes "which cannot be charmed". These words recall the story in Num. 21:6–9 where Moses prays to God on behalf of the people when they are attacked by venomous snakes. He is told to erect a bronze snake which counteracts the deadly venom in anyone who looks at it. But now there is no effective antidote. The venom must do its deadly work.

In between these two pictures of judgement we hear the people giving voice to their despair. Hoped-for peace, *shalom*, has proved illusory. There is no respite from the enemy. The prospect is death; the choice to die one by one where they are or to die huddled together in the fortified cities. There is no heroism here, like that of the Jews who died by their own hands in the last defiant stand against the Romans at Masada, but only black despair.

Read again 4:19–26, and the comments made there, as a background to 8:18–9:1. The prophet hears echoing through the land two incredulous questions:

Is the Lord not in Zion?
Is her King not in her? (verse 19)

The implications of Jeremiah's unpopular Temple Sermon (7:1–15), ignored at the time, are beginning to sink in. Perhaps after all the unthinkable is happening. These questions are capped by a question from the Lord who in effect says to the people "<u>Yes, I am present</u>; <u>so much the worse for you since you have provoked me to anger</u>".

Jeremiah's preaching is being vindicated, but he takes no pleasure in what is happening. He is filled with an unbearable sadness (verse 18). His people's agony is his agony; their wound is his wound, their grief his grief. Desperately he searches for a cure: "Is there no balm in Gilead?" (verse 22). The caravans that journeyed south from Damascus to Egypt carried various aromatic substances, some of which, including "balm", were believed to have medicinal properties. They entered Israel through the territory of Gilead. No cure from that quarter; no doctor; the people remain unhealed. For most of us the temptation to turn to the people and say "I told you so" would have been irresistible: Jeremiah could only weep bitter, solitary tears. These tears tell us as much about Jeremiah as the stern, uncompromising realism of his preaching.

THE PROPHET IN DESPAIR

Jeremiah 9:2–11

²O that I had in the desert
    a wayfarers' lodging place,
that I might leave my people
    and go away from them!
For they are all adulterers,
    a company of treacherous men.
³They bend their tongue like a bow;
    falsehood and not truth has grown strong in the land;
for they proceed from evil to evil,
    and they do not know me, says the Lord.

⁴Let every one beware of his neighbour,
    and put no trust in any brother;
for every brother is a supplanter,
    and every neighbour goes about as a slanderer.
⁵Every one deceives his neighbour,
    and no one speaks the truth;
they have taught their tongue to speak lies;
    they commit iniquity and are too weary to repent.
⁶Heaping oppression upon oppression, and deceit upon deceit,
    they refuse to know me, says the Lord.

⁷Therefore thus says the Lord of hosts:
    "Behold, I will refine them and test them,

for what else can I do, because of my people?
⁸Their tongue is a deadly arrow;
  it speaks deceitfully;
 with his mouth each speaks peaceably to his neighbour,
  but in his heart he plans an ambush for him.
⁹Shall I not punish them for these things? says the Lord;
  and shall I not avenge myself
  on a nation such as this?

¹⁰"Take up weeping and wailing for the mountains,
  and a lamentation for the pastures of the wilderness,
 because they are laid waste so that no one passes through,
  and the lowing of cattle is not heard;
 both the birds of the air and the beasts
  have fled and are gone.
¹¹I will make Jerusalem a heap of ruins,
  a lair of jackals;
 and I will make the cities of Judah a desolation,
  without inhabitant."

Tears were not the prophet's only response. He recoils in horror from the depravity he sees all around him. His natural instinct is to opt out of the corrupt society. A rough traveller's bothy in the back of beyond would be preferable to the luxury and decadence of the society life he knew (verse 2). To opt out would have been easy. Yet Jeremiah did not take that easy way. He stayed to share the suffering which his people's depravity made inevitable; and because he stayed he had a word to say to them in their darkest hour. Nowhere does the Bible encourage us to believe that we can find or serve God by withdrawing from his world and from our fellow men into some private oasis of personal spirituality. I John 4:20 sums this up when it says: "He who does not love his brother whom he has seen, cannot love God whom he has not seen". The trouble is, of course, that sometimes it is easier to love someone you have not seen than to love those you do see—they can be awkward, they can represent so many of the things of which you disapprove.

The nature of the people's depravity, indicated in very general terms in verse 2 by describing them all as adulterers and a gang of traitors, is spelled out in two brief sections, each ending in words which point to the real root of their trouble:

> They do not know me, says the Lord. (verse 3)
> They refuse to know me, says the Lord. (verse 6)

Such knowing for the Old Testament is never merely head knowledge: it is a relationship with God which is meaningless unless it is lived out in our relationships with one another (see comment on 2:8).

The people do not know the Lord because theirs is a society in which trust has broken down, where words have been devalued and where the tongue has become the instrument of hurting, insidious lies (verses 4–5, 8). The letter of James has some strong things to say about the damage that can be inflicted by a lying tongue (e.g. James 3:5ff.). The book of Proverbs lists seven things as abhorrent to the Lord:

> Haughty eyes, a lying tongue,
>   and hands that shed innocent blood,
> a heart that devises wicked plans,
>   feet that make haste to run to evil,
> a false witness who breathes out lies,
>   and a man who sows discord among brothers. (Prov. 6:17–18)

It reads like a paraphrase of what Jeremiah is saying here.

The words translated "for every brother is a supplanter" (verse 4) take us back to Gen. 27:36 where Esau, who has just been cheated out of his birthright by Jacob, bitterly says, "Is he not rightly named Jacob?", linking the name Jacob with the Hebrew verb *'aqab* which means to supplant or to cheat. Jacob the cheat: and his descendants were acting true to his character, out-Jacob-ing Jacob. Faced with this situation God has no choice. Into the crucible of suffering and humiliation the people must go, with God himself assuming the role he assigned to the prophet in 6:27, that of the refiner of his people (verse 7).

Jeremiah's response is to break into a lament (verse 10)—it is better to follow the Hebrew text at the beginning of verse 10 and read "I will take up weeping" (see the RSV footnote)—a lament evoked by the silence of death which has descended upon the countryside from the highlands to the desert steppe. His lament is interrupted by a further word from the Lord, confirming that his purpose is destructive: Jerusalem and the cities of Judah to become uninhabited ruins, the haunt of wolves.

The humanity, the sensitivity of Jeremiah shines through this and many other passages. Here is a man struggling to come to terms with conflicting emotions and loyalties; recoiling in horror from the depravity of his people, yet unable to leave them; convinced of the rightness of God's word of judgement upon his people, yet greeting its coming, not with exultation, but with a lament.

A TIME FOR MOURNING

Jeremiah 9:12–22

12Who is the man so wise that he can understand this? To whom has the mouth of the Lord spoken, that he may declare it? Why is the land ruined and laid waste like a wilderness, so that no one passes through? 13And the Lord says: "Because they have forsaken my law which I set before them, and have not obeyed my voice, or walked in accord with it, 14but have stubbornly followed their own hearts and have gone after the Baals, as their fathers taught them. 15Therefore thus says the Lord of hosts, the God of Israel: Behold, I will feed this people with wormwood, and give them poisonous water to drink. 16I will scatter them among the nations whom neither they nor their fathers have known; and I will send the sword after them, until I have consumed them."

17Thus says the Lord of hosts:
   "Consider, and call for the mourning women to come;
      send for the skilful women to come;
18let them make haste and raise a wailing over us,
      that our eyes may run down with tears,
      and our eyelids gush with water.
19For a sound of wailing is heard from Zion:
      'How we are ruined!
      We are utterly shamed,

because we have left the land,
    because they have cast down our dwellings.'"

²⁰Hear, O women, the word of the Lord,
    and let your ear receive the word of his mouth;
teach to your daughters a lament,
    and each to her neighbour a dirge.
²¹For death has come up into our windows,
    it has entered our palaces,
cutting off the children from the streets
    and the young men from the squares.
²²Speak, "Thus says the Lord:
'The dead bodies of men shall fall
    like dung upon the open field,
like sheaves after the reaper,
    and none shall gather them.'"

Verses 12–16 constitute another of these little sermons in the language and style of Deuteronomy which provide further commentary on the teaching of Jeremiah. After an introduction which stresses that a true, wise understanding of what has happened can only come from someone in touch with God, the passage (a) asks a question (verse 12), (b) answers the question (verses 13–14) and (c) underlines the circumstances which give rise to the question (verse 15). The question which haunted the religious consciousness of the Jews, after the destruction of the city they thought indestructible, was "Why did it happen?" The answer, in line with all prophetic teaching in the Old Testament, is the people's disloyalty to God. Out of this comes the bitter experience of exile to distant lands and death. The bitterness of their fate is underlined by the reference in verse 15 to "wormwood", a plant whose juice had a very bitter taste, and to "poisonous water", the juice of a noxious herb, often translated "gall" (cf. Lam. 3:19), which seeded itself in the fields. Many a sermon must have been preached to the exiles on this theme, and during the Exile the history of Israel which runs from 1 Samuel to 2 Kings was edited to illustrate its truth. You will find another similar sermon in 16:10–13. Whoever wrote these little sermons, they are true to Jeremiah's account of the deep-seated religious malaise which sealed the nation's fate.

After the little prose interlude the poetry of mourning is resumed (verses 17–22).

We have listened to Jeremiah's personal lament in verse 10; now the call goes out to the professional mourning women who, in many ancient societies, accompany the funeral procession with their high-pitched keening and wailing. But the totality of the devastation in Zion is beyond the resources of these mourning women on their own; they have to teach their skills to their daughters and neighbours. Verse 21 provides us with a good example of a lament, Hebrew *qinah*, with its characteristic line of three stresses followed by a shorter line of two stresses. We get something of the flavour of this if we translate:

> Death has climbed in through our windows,
>> entered our palaces,
> cutting off children in the streets,
>> young folk in the squares.

To this picture of death the sneak-thief, stealing into homes and stalking the streets, there is added in verse 22 the picture of death the grim reaper, a metaphor which has a long literary history and appears in several of Longfellow's poems:

> There is a Reaper, whose name is Death,
>> And, with his sickle keen,
> He reaps the bearded grain at a breath,
>> And the flowers that grow between.
>>> *The Reaper and the Flowers*

This grim reaper's harvest is the corpses which lie ungathered in the fields, since there is no one left to bury them (cf. 8:2). Such sombre notes are to be heard again in 10:17–25, but before that there is what could be called an intermission in three parts.

INTERMISSION (i)

Jeremiah 9:23–10:16

²³Thus says the Lord: "Let not the wise man glory in his wisdom, let not the mighty man glory in his might, let not the rich man glory in his

riches; [24]but let him who glories glory in this, that he understands and knows me, that I am the Lord who practise steadfast love, justice, and righteousness in the earth; for in these things I delight, says the Lord."

[25]"Behold, the days are coming, says the Lord, when I will punish all those who are circumcised but yet uncircumcised—[26]Egypt, Judah, Edom, the sons of Ammon, Moab, and all who dwell in the desert that cut the corners of their hair; for all these nations are uncircumcised, and all the house of Israel is uncircumcised in heart."

[1]Hear the word which the Lord speaks to you, O house of Israel.
[2]Thus says the Lord:
"Learn not the way of the nations,
    nor be dismayed at the signs of the heavens
    because the nations are dismayed at them,
[3]for the customs of the peoples are false.
A tree from the forest is cut down,
    and worked with an axe by the hands of a craftsman.
[4]Men deck it with silver and gold;
    they fasten it with hammer and nails
    so that it cannot move.
[5]Their idols are like scarecrows in a cucumber field,
    and they cannot speak;
they have to be carried,
    for they cannot walk.
Be not afraid of them,
    for they cannot do evil,
    neither is it in them to do good."

[6]There is none like thee, O Lord;
    thou art great, and thy name is great in might.
[7]Who would not fear thee, O King of the nations?
    For this is thy due;
for among all the wise ones of the nations
    and in all their kingdoms
    there is none like thee.
[8]They are both stupid and foolish;
    the instruction of idols is but wood!
[9]Beaten silver is brought from Tarshish,
    and gold from Uphaz.
They are the work of the craftsman and of the hands of the goldsmith;

their clothing is violet and purple;
they are all the work of skilled men.
¹⁰But the Lord is the true God;
he is the living God and the everlasting King.
At his wrath the earth quakes,
and the nations cannot endure his indignation.

¹¹Thus shall you say to them: "The gods who did not make the heavens and the earth shall perish from the earth and from under the heavens."

¹²It is he who made the earth by his power,
who established the world by his wisdom,
and by his understanding stretched out the heavens.
¹³When he utters his voice there is a tumult of waters in the heavens,
and he makes the mist rise from the ends of the earth.
He makes lightnings for the rain,
and he brings forth the wind from his storehouses.

¹⁴Every man is stupid and without knowledge;
every goldsmith is put to shame by his idols;
for his images are false,
and there is no breath in them.
¹⁵They are worthless, a work of delusion;
at the time of their punishment they shall perish.
¹⁶Not like these is he who is the portion of Jacob,
for he is the one who formed all things,
and Israel is the tribe of his inheritance;
the Lord of hosts is his name.

The three parts of the intermission are:

(1) *True Grounds for Boasting* (9:23–24). Just as Jeremiah's lament in 9:10–11 is followed by a discussion about what true wisdom or understanding means, so the lament in 9:17–22 leads into a passage centring upon that wisdom of which people may be rightly proud. It is not mere human skill or prowess, nor a substantial bank balance, but that knowledge of the Lord which expresses itself in action, in a life which reflects the way God acts in "steadfast love" (Hebrew *hesed*; see comment on 2:2), "justice and righteousness" (see comment on 4:1–2). For the Bible there is no one set of rules which we can keep and say that's it, that

is what God requires of me. There is something far more demanding, a vision of God, a picture of the way *he* acts, and the challenge to live in the light of that. So in the book of Leviticus we hear it in the words "You shall be holy; for I the Lord your God am holy" (Lev. 19:2); and on the lips of Jesus "You, therefore, must be perfect as your heavenly Father is perfect" (Matt. 5:48). It is daunting, uncompromisingly demanding, indeed unattainable, yet it can be faced because it comes to us in the context of God's steadfast love.

(2) *Pagan Israel* (9:25–26). These verses pick up again the theme of 4:4, the difference between circumcision as an outward physical sign, and the true circumcision which must be that of the heart. Other nations surrounding Israel practised circumcision, and some of them are listed in verse 26. The reference to those who "cut the corners of their hair" probably alludes to shaving part of the head in what Israel thought of as pagan rites linked with mourning for the dead (see Lev. 19:27; not therefore the normal shaving of the head mentioned in 7:29). But Israel herself is no better than such pagans, circumcised but not "in heart", and therefore equally vulnerable to God's punishment. It is easy to dismiss others as pagan or irreligious, but far more difficult to face the paganism in ourselves. The more we claim to be religious, the more we ought to ponder the deadly serious humour of Jesus: "Why do you see the speck that is in your brother's eye, but do not notice the log that is in your own eye?" (Matt. 7:3).

INTERMISSION (ii)

Jeremiah 9:23–10:16 *(cont'd)*

(3) *The One True God.* Are not all religions really the same? Does it matter what we call God or how we worship him as long as we believe in some higher power beyond ourselves? Many people in Israel must have asked such questions, as many do today. The prophet's answer is to be found in 10:1–16. It is a difficult passage. It is one of the sections in the book where the Greek text differs considerably from the standard Hebrew text followed by

our English versions. Many scholars believe that it comes from a
time later than Jeremiah, from the period of the Exile, and point
to the close links with the teaching of the anonymous prophet of
the Exile who wrote Isaiah chapters 40–55; see, for example, Isa.
40:18–20; 44:9–20; 46:5–7. Yet these links are not always as close
as our English translations suggest. There is no reason why this
passage could not come from Jeremiah. A section of it, verses
12–16, appears again in the book of Jeremiah as 51:15–19, while
verse 11 is in Aramaic; perhaps it is the comment of a later scribe;
if so it is a very appropriate comment. Beyond all the questions it
raises, however, the passage presents us with two skilfully inter-
woven and sharply contrasting themes which are important for
biblical faith:

(i) poking fun at the futility of the worship of other gods
    (verses 2–5, 8–9, 14–15)
(ii) celebrating the wonder and the power of Israel's own real
    God (verses 6–7, 12–13, 16).

(i) "Poor misguided fools", that is the verdict on those who
follow "the way of the nations" (verse 2). They are in on astrol-
ogy: plotting the movement of the stars and the planets, assessing
the influence of any unusual "signs" in the heavens that may bear
on human life. They make idols. No expense is spared. Craftsmen
skilfully use gold and silver imported from distant lands. The net
result is mere objects, aesthetically pleasing but dead, as dead as
a dodo or, as verse 5 graphically puts it, standing "like scarecrows
in a cucumber field", unable to speak, unable to move, unable to
do anything. Can this really be what God is like?

Now we can imagine a worshipper who used such idols reply-
ing: "That's unfair comment; we don't worship such images; they
are no more than helpful symbols of the gods we worship". True
enough, but this passage is not written to convert such people; its
purpose is to confirm the prophet's own people in their commitment to the One who, in the words of verse 10, is "the living
God", the God who is ever active. How can a dead, lifeless piece
of wood or metal be an adequate symbol of such a living God?
Particularly within the Protestant tradition we are quick to say

"Amen, brother, no graven images!" Perhaps we ought to stop and ask ourselves whether there is not a danger that the *words* we use may not equally be such images, dead, lifeless images in which we may imprison the living God, not least when we insist that those who do not use the same words as we do must be in error.

(ii) True faith, on the contrary, means celebration. This note of celebration is sounded in several hymn-like verses—they may indeed be extracts from hymns. They celebrate the wonder of this living God, unique in his power over all nations (verses 6–7), creator of the universe, controller of all the forces in it (verses 12–13), king (verse 10), yet no aloof monarch, but one to whom Israel is bound in an intimate relationship of his making (verse 16). This is what is meant by describing God as "the portion of Jacob", and Israel as "the tribe of his inheritance". These are dangerous phrases. They could be—and were—twisted to mean "God belongs to us"; they are meant to mean "we belong to God". There is a difference. The one leads to people using God for their own purposes, claiming a monopoly interest in him; the other leads to commitment to God's service. The one was the misunderstanding that blinded many people in Jerusalem in Jeremiah's day; the other was the stance of the prophet. It was to destroy this misunderstanding that "God belongs to us" that the people had to be thrown out of the false security of their city of God into the cold and bitter experience of exile. This is the theme which is developed in the next daily portion.

TRAGEDY AND RESPONSE

Jeremiah 10:17–25

> 17Gather up your bundle from the ground,
>   O you who dwell under siege!
> 18For thus says the Lord:
>   "Behold, I am slinging out the inhabitants of the land
>   at this time,

and I will bring distress on them,
and they may feel it."

19Woe is me because of my hurt!
My wound is grievous.
But I said, "Truly this is an affliction,
and I must bear it."
20My tent is destroyed,
and all my cords are broken;
my children have gone from me,
and they are not;
there is no one to spread my tent again,
and to set up my curtains.
21For the shepherds are stupid,
and do not inquire of the Lord;
therefore they have not prospered,
and all their flock is scattered.

22Hark, a rumour! Behold, it comes!—
a great commotion out of the north country
to make the cities of Judah a desolation,
a lair of jackals.

23I know, O Lord, that the way of man is not in himself,
that it is not in man who walks to direct his steps.
24Correct me, O Lord, but in just measure;
not in thy anger, lest thou bring me to nothing.

25Pour out thy wrath upon the nations that know thee not,
and upon the peoples that call not on thy name;
for they have devoured Jacob;
they have devoured him and consumed him,
and have laid waste his habitation.

The coming fate of the people is briefly and dramatically described in verses 17–18. They are to be slung out of the land. The threatening foe from the north is in action (verse 22). Part of the blame for this is laid squarely on the shoulders of "the shepherds", the rulers who played power politics instead of seeking to know and to do God's will: so their flock, the nation, is scattered (verse 21). But, as in all tragedy, much depends on how people respond to it. The same tragedy that breaks one person, may make another. We find here a two-fold response:

(1) There is the immediate response contained in the lament in verses 19–20. It is the response of heart-broken acceptance of something that cannot be changed:

Truly this is an affliction, and I must bear it. (verse 19)

These may be the words of Jerusalem speaking as a mother bereft of her children, her home destroyed; or they may be the words of Jeremiah identifying himself with the people in their tragedy. There can be courage and nobility in such an attitude of acceptance, particularly if it is that realistic acceptance summed up in the prayer "God grant me the serenity to accept the things that I cannot change, the courage to change the things I can, and the wisdom to know the difference".

(2) This attitude of acceptance—and here it is the prophet who is speaking—draws strength from acknowledging that man is not the master of his own destiny. There is no such thing as a self-made man (verse 23). In many ways the course of his life is not his to decide. This could be a terrifying thought unless, as verse 24 assumes, we are in the hands of a God who may indeed have to discipline us, but who can be relied upon to do so not irresponsibly but justly. If this be so then the response to tragedy is prayer which accepts our human limitations and frailty and reaches out to a God who can be trusted even in the darkest hour.

Verse 25 is also found in Ps. 79:6–7, a psalm of national lament. Many scholars believe that this prayer does not come from Jeremiah but was added later from the psalm, which reflects the embittered attitude of the exiles towards the pagan foreigners who had destroyed their homeland. This may be so. But to dismiss it, however, as merely a reflection of a narrow religious nationalism is to miss a point which is central to the thinking of all the psalmists and all the prophets, not least Jeremiah. For them the God of Israel is the lord of all nations, and all nations are accountable to him for callous abuse of power and for the atrocities they commit—see Amos chapter 1 and the oracles against the nations in Jeremiah chapters 46–51.

E. THE MAN OF ACTION...AND INNER CONFLICTS (CHS. 11–20)

Chapters 1–10 deal mainly with the message of Jeremiah, whether that message comes to us in brief poetic passages or in the longer prose sermons. Only one section describes an incident in the life of Jeremiah, the unpopular Temple Sermon in 7:1–15. In chapters 11–20 the balance changes. There is still the same message, uncompromising in its challenge and its realism. The people have rejected the Lord; they are reaping the bitter harvest of their own folly (12:7–13; 15:1–9). The die is now irrevocably cast, the time for prayer is over (11:14; 14:11–12). Two other elements, however, are far more strongly represented in chapters 11–20 than in chapters 1–10.

(1) There are several passages which claim to describe incidents in Jeremiah's career as a prophet. Some deal with public sermons the prophet is called to preach: the sermon on "the curse of the broken covenant" (11:1–8), the sermon at the Benjamin Gate on "sabbath observance" (17:19–27). Others centre upon what have been called symbolic acts, things that the prophet did at the Lord's command. They are like acted parables which either fix in the prophet's mind the message God wishes to give him or dramatically convey that message to the people. Thus there are the incidents involving a ruined loincloth (13:1–11), the command to remain celibate (16:1–9), the visit to the potter's workshop (18:1–12), the smashing of the jar at the Potsherd's Gate (19:1–13). We shall have more to say about the significance of such symbolic acts when we look at the first of them, the ruined loincloth, in chapter 13. Most of these incidents have been written up by editors, but they are rooted in authentic experiences of the prophet. They help us to sketch in Jeremiah's profile, but we are left guessing when they happened since none of them is dated.

(2) We have already had occasion to note passages in which something of Jeremiah's inner feelings surface, as he contemplates coming tragedy (see the comments on 4:19; 8:18ff.). It

is within chapters 11–20, however, that we find most of the material which makes up Jeremiah's spiritual diary (see Introduction). Here we are brought face to face with what was for Jeremiah the harsh and inevitable cost of being a prophet, just as the agony in the garden of Gethsemane and the cry of dereliction on the cross spring from Jesus' faithfulness to his ministry. And if in these passages we hear no "Father forgive" but only a bitter "forgive not", let not those of us who so often remain carefully in the spiritual shallows be quick to sit in judgement on the prophet's cries from the deep. There are parallels in thought and language between such passages and some of the most intensely personal of the Psalms which give voice to perplexity and doubt (see, for example, Psalms 3, 17 and 73). The Jeremiah passages, however, have a character of their own, for they are closely related to his sense of vocation; they also help us to bridge the gulf between what often seems the cold assurance of a man who says "Thus says the Lord" and the kind of spiritual problems and uncertainties with which we ourselves often have to wrestle.

THE BROKEN COVENANT AND ITS DIRE CONSEQUENCES

Jeremiah 11:1–17

¹The word that came to Jeremiah from the Lord: ²"Hear the words of this covenant, and speak to the men of Judah and the inhabitants of Jerusalem. ³You shall say to them, Thus says the Lord, the God of Israel: Cursed be the man who does not heed the words of this covenant ⁴which I commanded your fathers when I brought them out of the land of Egypt, from the iron furnace, saying, Listen to my voice, and do all that I command you. So shall you be my people, and I will be your God, ⁵that I may perform the oath which I swore to your fathers, to give them a land flowing with milk and honey, as at this day." Then I answered, "So be it, Lord."

⁶And the Lord said to me, "Proclaim all these words in the cities of Judah, and in the streets of Jerusalem: Hear the words of this covenant

and do them. [7]For I solemnly warned your fathers when I brought them up out of the land of Egypt, warning them persistently, even to this day, saying, Obey my voice. [8]Yet they did not obey or incline their ear, but every one walked in the stubbornness of his evil heart. Therefore I brought upon them all the words of this covenant, which I commanded them to do, but they did not."

[9]Again the Lord said to me, "There is revolt among the men of Judah and the inhabitants of Jerusalem. [10]They have turned back to the iniquities of their forefathers, who refused to hear my words; they have gone after other gods to serve them; the house of Israel and the house of Judah have broken my covenant which I made with their fathers. [11]Therefore, thus says the Lord, Behold, I am bringing evil upon them which they cannot escape; though they cry to me, I will not listen to them. [12]Then the cities of Judah and the inhabitants of Jerusalem will go and cry to the gods to whom they burn incense, but they cannot save them in the time of their trouble. [13]For your gods have become as many as your cities, O Judah; and as many as the streets of Jerusalem are the altars you have set up to shame, altars to burn incense to Baal.

[14]"Therefore do not pray for this people, or lift up a cry or prayer on their behalf, for I will not listen when they call to me in the time of their trouble. [15]What right has my beloved in my house, when she has done vile deeds? Can vows and sacrificial flesh avert your doom? Can you then exult? [16]The Lord once called you, 'A green olive tree, fair with goodly fruit'; but with the roar of a great tempest he will set fire to it, and its branches will be consumed. [17]The Lord of hosts, who planted you, has pronounced evil against you, because of the evil which the house of Israel and the house of Judah have done, provoking me to anger by burning incense to Baal."

The prophet is commanded to go on a preaching mission, to repeat to the people "the words of this covenant", a key phrase which occurs four times in this passage, in verses 2,3,6 and 8. It makes most sense if "the words of *this* covenant" refer to a significant contemporary event, the renewal of the covenant relationship with the Lord into which King Josiah led his people in the national reformation of 621 B.C. We do not know for certain what Jeremiah's attitude to the reformation was. The words of this passage do not necessarily mean that prior to the reformation he acted as an itinerant evangelist calling upon people to respond to the reformation call. They might equally well mean that after the reformation Jeremiah, seeing that it was failing to bite, called upon the people to take seriously that call to reform to which they had paid only lip service.

The covenant of 621 B.C. did not, of course, claim to be a new covenant; it claimed to be a renewal of the original covenant between the Lord and Israel as that is described for us in the book of Deuteronomy. The basic purpose of that covenant was to establish a relationship summed up in the words "So shall you be my people, and I will be your God" (verse 4). The move to establish that relationship came from God—he brought the people out of slavery in Egypt. It was a relationship which looked in hope to a future which would see the fulfilment of God's promises and a prosperous life for the people (verse 5). But it was a relationship which laid upon the people serious obligations to live as God's people in obedience to his will. Failure to do so would bring an inevitable curse. Look up Deut. 27:15–26 and you will find a series of such curses, culminating in the general statement "Cursed be he who does not confirm the words of this law by doing them" (Deut. 27:26). To each curse proclaimed by Moses the people respond "Amen"—so be it. Jeremiah recalls the curse (verse 3) and responds "Amen"— "So be it, Lord" (verse 5).

Such was the covenant relationship as it was intended to be. But Israel's past history was the story of a relationship which had turned sour, because of the failure of the people to give that kind of obedience for which God looked (verses 6–8). As for the present, claims Jeremiah, it is but the past all over again, the same sorry story of a nation in "revolt" (verse 9), mounting, as it were, a conspiracy against God. The only kind of turning (*shuv*) they are interested in is a turning back to the sins of their forefathers (verse 10). The cities of Judah played host to many cults (verse 13). Religion was big business; no doubt it could have bought prime time on TV if that had been available. But the people are in deep trouble, staring in the face disaster from "which they cannot escape" (verse 11). The curse of the covenant is on them. They would have been better not to have been the people of God, than to be a people who played fast and loose with God. It was as true of Israel, as it still is of us that, in the words of Jesus, "Every one to whom much is given, of him will much be required" (Luke 12:48). The time for prayer either by the prophet on behalf of the people or by the people themselves is over. It is too late; God is no longer listening (verse 14).

It is a grim picture, yet it should have been different. We catch a glimpse of what might have been in two descriptions of the people in verses 15 and 16:

(1) *my beloved* (verse 15; cf. 12:7); they are still the Lord's beloved in spite of what they have done and are still doing. The story of Israel is thus the story of a prodigal son who will not or cannot come to his senses; but waiting, hoping, there is still a loving father.

(2) *a green olive tree* (verse 16), beautiful, planted by God, planted in the expectation that it would go on bearing fruit; but now, sadly, about to be ravaged by fire.

"What might have been" can be a depressing comment on life, unless there are grounds for hoping that, in spite of everything, what might have been can still be. To have the story of Israel presented to us as the story of a broken covenant and its dire consequences is to be left asking "Does this mean that God has finally slammed the door in the face of Israel, or can that door still be kept open?" Is there a possibility of new life beyond the impending holocaust? Other passages in the book of Jeremiah, notably in chapters 30–33, have something to say in answer to such questions.

THE COST OF BEING A PROPHET

Jeremiah 11:18–12:6

¹⁸The Lord made it known to me and I knew;
    then thou didst show me their evil deeds.
¹⁹But I was like a gentle lamb
    led to the slaughter.

I did not know it was against me
 they devised schemes, saying,
"Let us destroy the tree with its fruit,
 let us cut him off from the land of the living,
 that his name be remembered no more."
²⁰But, O Lord of hosts, who judgest righteously,
 who triest the heart and the mind,
let me see thy vengeance upon them,
 for to thee have I committed my cause.

²¹Therefore thus says the Lord concerning the men of Anathoth, who seek your life, and say, "Do not prophesy in the name of the Lord, or you will die by our hand"—²²therefore thus says the Lord of hosts: "Behold, I will punish them; the young men shall die by the sword; their sons and their daughters shall die by famine; ²³and none of them shall be left. For I will bring evil upon the men of Anathoth, the year of their punishment."

¹Righteous art thou, O Lord, when I complain to thee;
 yet I would plead my case before thee.
Why does the way of the wicked prosper?
 Why do all who are treacherous thrive?
²Thou plantest them, and they take root;
 they grow and bring forth fruit;
thou art near in their mouth
 and far from their heart.
³But thou, O Lord, knowest me;
 thou seest me, and triest my mind toward thee.
Pull them out like sheep for the slaughter,
 and set them apart for the day of slaughter.
⁴How long will the land mourn,
 and the grass of every field wither?
For the wickedness of those who dwell in it
 the beasts and the birds are swept away,
 because men said, "He will not see our latter end."

⁵"If you have raced with men on foot, and they have wearied you,
 how will you compete with horses?
And if in a safe land you fall down,
 how will you do in the jungle of the Jordan?
⁶For even your brothers and the house of your father,

> even they have dealt treacherously with you;
>   they are in full cry after you;
> believe them not,
>   though they speak fair words to you."

This is the first in a series of passages which read like extracts from Jeremiah's spiritual diary. They show us something of the man behind the message. Let us notice first of all what kind of passages these are. They are not the work of a man jotting down his own thoughts and feelings in a notebook. They are not Shakespearean soliloquies where words reveal unspoken dreams and inner conflicts. In the main they are prayers, prayers often startlingly raw in their honesty and candour, prayers which, far from being the expression of calm assurance and certain faith, pour out perplexity and hatred to God. Sometimes the prayers are answered by a word from the Lord to the prophet; sometimes there is no answer.

This section falls into two parts: (1) 11:18–23 and (2) 12:1–6, each of them containing a prayer from the prophet and an answering word from the Lord. How these two parts fit together has been much discussed. The first section assumes that Jeremiah knew of a plot against him by his kinsmen in Anathoth, while 12:6 implies that he did not know. Some scholars have argued that for this reason 12:1–6 ought to come before 11:18–23. However we answer this problem, both parts deal with opposition which came to Jeremiah in the course of his ministry, and tell us something about how he reacted.

(1) 11:18–23. Here is opposition which apparently took the prophet by surprise. He describes himself as being "like a gentle lamb led to the slaughter" (verse 19). You will find the same words used in a famous passage in Isa. 53:7 to describe the suffering servant of the Lord. This is only one among many indications that the experience of Jeremiah may have contributed to the portrait of the servant which we find in Isaiah chapters 40ff.

Yet the same words can often mean different things. In Isa. 53:7 the words are used to describe how the servant was led like a lamb to the slaughter and all the while remained silent, accepting his fate without protest. Jeremiah, as we shall see, was anything but silent in the face of opposition. Bitter words of protest were often on his lips. The picture of the "gentle lamb" is used here to indicate that what happened to Jeremiah took him by surprise. Before he knew what was happening, they were out to get him: "I did not know it was against me they devised schemes . . ." (verse 19). If others are against him, what about God? He turns in confidence to the Lord as to a fair-minded judge who must give right decisions, who examines the hidden thoughts and intentions of men, and who can be depended upon to acquit his servant and thwart his accusers (verse 20). The Lord's reply in verses 21–23 assumes that Jeremiah's confidence is not misplaced. His enemies will be punished, caught up in the dire fate which is going to engulf the whole nation.

There remains, however, a puzzle. Why should Jeremiah have been treated as a social leper by his fellow-villagers? Why were "the men of Anathoth" determined to liquidate him and to silence his prophetic word? We do not know. There have been many guesses. Perhaps the clue lies in the fact that this passage comes immediately after the account of Jeremiah's preaching mission in support of the covenant. As part of the reformation of 621 B.C. worship was to be centralised in the Temple at Jerusalem. All local shrines, which too easily became centres of superstition and corruption, were to be closed. Suppose that Jeremiah, the local lad who apparently had become too big for his boots, appeared in Anathoth supporting the closure of what was the local church. Anyone who has had anything to do with church unions and readjustments knows only too well the angry response which any proposal to close "our church" receives. More generally, the savage attacks which Jeremiah had made upon the social and religious corruption of his people meant that he was a highly controversial and unpopular figure. Perhaps his fellow-villagers thought that something of this unpopularity might rub off on themselves. They would disassociate themselves from his attitude: either he had to be persuaded to stop preaching such radical nonsense, or they would silence him.

(2) 12:1–6. To have confidence in God, however, does not

mean that all problems are solved. Jeremiah has a problem. He takes it to the divine judge, a "righteous" judge, that is a judge who can be relied upon to give right decisions. The problem is this: "Why does the way of the wicked prosper?" (12:1).

It is an age-old problem, and one that was increasingly to perplex the faithful in Israel; witness Psalm 73 and the book of Job. According to a widely-held belief in ancient Israel, a belief you will see set out in Psalm 1, the wicked do not prosper; it is only the righteous who take root and become a fruitful tree. But Jeremiah's experience—and the experience of countless folk ever since—pointed in the opposite direction. His whole energy had been poured out in God's service—as God well knew (verse 3)—and the result had been rejection and persecution. Yet those who rejected and persecuted him, and paid no attention to the word of God, flourished. To cry for vengeance, to say that it is they who ought to be dragged off like sheep to the slaughter-house, is understandable (verse 3), but it still leaves unanswered that stubborn question "Why . . . why should things work out like this in a God-controlled world?" And if we have never been haunted by that question, we have never begun to think.

As so often in life, however, the question "why?" is not really a plea for a neat, intellectually-satisfying answer. It is something much more basic: a cry for help. How can I cope? In Jeremiah's case, how in face of virulent and successful opposition and seeming personal failure, how can I continue with my prophetic mission? It is to meet this problem that the answer comes in verses 5–6. It may at first seem a strange answer. In a nutshell what the Lord says to Jeremiah is this: cheer up . . . there is worse to come! If you are finding the going tough, it is going to get tougher. If you are stumbling already "in a safe land" (verse 5), in the open countryside, what is going to happen "in the jungle of Jordan", the tropical thickets in the Jordan valley, home in Old Testament times of marauding lions (49:19) and therefore a symbol of danger? To change slightly the metaphor at the beginning of verse 5, "If you can't jog a mile, what is going to happen when you run in the marathon?" Jeremiah seems to have been tempted to give up too soon.

Although the reply may seem cold comfort, it does speak to Jeremiah's spiritual problem. It assumes that he can, that he must, that he *will* continue his prophetic ministry into even stormier days ahead. To believe in God when the sun is shining and all is going well, that is easy, but to believe when the storm clouds gather and the going is hard, that is the test of faith. Jeremiah was being challenged to hold on in the midst of ever-increasing difficulties, to hold on to the promise made to him at his call: "For I am with you to deliver you, says the Lord" (1:8). That makes sense, even when many questions remain unanswered, as they do for all of us.

THE LORD OF ALL NATIONS

Jeremiah 12:7–17

7"I have forsaken my house,
　　I have abandoned my heritage;
　I have given the beloved of my soul
　　into the hands of her enemies.
8My heritage has become to me
　　like a lion in the forest,
　she has lifted up her voice against me;
　　therefore I hate her.
9Is my heritage to me like a speckled bird of prey?
　　Are the birds of prey against her round about?
　Go, assemble all the wild beasts;
　　bring them to devour.
10Many shepherds have destroyed my vineyard,
　　they have trampled down my portion,
　they have made my pleasant portion
　　a desolate wilderness.
11They have made it a desolation;
　　desolate, it mourns to me.
　The whole land is made desolate,
　　but no man lays it to heart.
12Upon all the bare heights in the desert
　　destroyers have come;

for the sword of the Lord devours
from one end of the land to the other;
no flesh has peace.
13They have sown wheat and have reaped thorns,
they have tired themselves out but profit nothing.
They shall be ashamed of their harvests
because of the fierce anger of the Lord."

14Thus says the Lord concerning all my evil neighbours who touch the heritage which I have given my people Israel to inherit: "Behold, I will pluck them up from their land, and I will pluck up the house of Judah from among them. 15And after I have plucked them up, I will again have compassion on them, and I will bring them again each to his heritage and each to his land. 16And it shall come to pass, if they will diligently learn the ways of my people, to swear by my name, 'As the Lord lives,' even as they taught my people to swear by Baal, then they shall be built up in the midst of my people. 17But if any nation will not listen, then I will utterly pluck it up and destroy it, says the Lord."

From Jeremiah's problem we turn to God's problem, as he laments the devastation which has befallen the nation. This divine lament may well reflect the events described in 2 Kings 24:1–2 when, as the result of King Jehoiakim's rebellion against his Babylonian overlord, marauding bands of Babylonian, Aramean, Moabite and Ammonite soldiers pillaged the Judean countryside. The tension in the lament is underlined in the opening verse, verse 7. This, says God, is "my house" (my people), the "beloved of my soul", "my heritage", but this I have been forced to desert, to abandon, to give into the hands of the enemy. It is as if God is torn between what he would have liked to do and what he is compelled to do by a people who have roared defiance in his face (verse 8). Defy God and the consequence is ruin. Israel has become like "a speckled bird of prey" (verse 9), attacked by other birds of prey; or, if we follow the Greek translation, like a hyena's den upon which vultures swoop to peck at the remains of the carcasses (see NEB).

Notice in verses 10 and 11 the four-fold occurrence of the words "desolate"/"desolation". This is but a pale reflection of the way in which in verse 11 in particular the Hebrew text plays upon the letters which make up the Hebrew word for desolation. Foreign rulers (shepherds) have spread desolation and devastation from one end of the land to the other. The fields lie untended, the seed sown, but the only harvest is thorns (verse 13). This is the price the people have paid; and it is the price God has to pay. The tensions in the lament point us to the fact that there is a cross in the heart of God before ever there was a cross on Calvary.

There are three central characters in the lament in verses 7–13, God, the people of God, and the other nations who act as God's destroying agents. It is the relationship between these three which is discussed in the prose section beginning at verse 14. Its teaching focuses on a key word, a word which occurs in the command to Jeremiah in 1:10, the word "pluck up" or "uproot"—see verses 14, 15 and 17.

(1) Other nations may be the agents God uses, but he has no illusions about them. They are "evil neighbours" (verse 14), power-crazed pagans. Therefore they in turn will be uprooted from their land. But the attitude to these "evil neighbours" is not entirely negative. They have a choice—as Israel always had a choice. They have tried to lead Israel away from her loyalty to the Lord, but they may yet become part of Israel "built up in the midst of my people" (verse 16), welcomed, as it were, into God's family provided they commit themselves to the worship of the God of Israel. The alternative to such conversion is that they will be completely uprooted and have no future.

(2) As for the people of God, Judah, she may look forward in hope to the day when she will be "uprooted" from the land to which she is going to be exiled. There will be a day of restoration. There are many passages in the book of Jeremiah which speak of such national restoration after the nation has gone through the refining fire of affliction (e.g. 16:14–15; 23:1–4).

This brief passage is, therefore, reminding us of truths that are of lasting importance in the thought of the Bible. Just because God's nature is described again and again in the Old Testament in terms of "steadfast love" (*hesed*; see 2:2) and compassion there must be hope in the midst of and beyond tragedy. God's last word is never "No"; not even "no" to those whom we too easily label his enemies. Although Israel's faith often moved within the confines of a narrow nationalism there were those who held on to a wider vision, a vision that included hope for all nations (see Isa. 2:2–4; Gen. 12:1–3). It is easier to say that, than to face the narrowness which often mars our vision.

THE SPOILED LINEN WAISTCLOTH

Jeremiah 13:1–14

[1]Thus said the Lord to me, "Go and buy a linen waistcloth, and put it on your loins, and do not dip it in water." [2]So I bought a waistcloth according to the word of the Lord, and put it on my loins. [3]And the word of the Lord came to me a second time, [4]"Take the waistcloth which you have bought, which is upon your loins, and arise, go to the Euphrates, and hide it there in a cleft of the rock." [5]So I went, and hid it by the Euphrates, as the Lord commanded me. [6]And after many days the Lord said to me, "Arise, go to the Euphrates, and take from there the waistcloth which I commanded you to hide there." [7]Then I went to the Euphrates, and dug, and I took the waistcloth from the place where I had hidden it. And behold, the waistcloth was spoiled; it was good for nothing.

[8]Then the word of the Lord came to me: [9]"Thus says the Lord: Even so will I spoil the pride of Judah and the great pride of Jerusalem. [10]This evil people, who refuse to hear my words, who stubbornly follow their own heart and have gone after other gods to serve them and worship them, shall be like this waistcloth, which is good for nothing. [11]For as the waistcloth clings to the loins of a man, so I made the whole house of Israel and the whole house of Judah cling to me, says the Lord, that they might be for me a people, a name, a praise, and a glory, but they would not listen.

[12]"You shall speak to them this word: 'Thus says the Lord, the God of Israel, "Every jar shall be filled with wine."' And they will say to you, 'Do we not indeed know that every jar will be filled with wine?' [13]Then

you shall say to them, 'Thus says the Lord: Behold, I will fill with drunkenness all the inhabitants of this land: the kings who sit on David's throne, the priests, the prophets, and all the inhabitants of Jerusalem. ¹⁴And I will dash them one against another, fathers and sons together, says the Lord. I will not pity or spare or have compassion, that I should not destroy them.'"

The incident related in verses 1–11 is the first of the "symbolic acts" attributed to Jeremiah in the book.

Such acts are not merely illustrations or visual aids. *They are the message*, the word in action. What the prophet did deliberately in obedience to God was not only a powerful way of communicating the message but a dramatic way of indicating that God's purposes, be they ominous or hopeful, were on their way to fulfilment. People might have found difficulty in remembering the finer details of the teaching of the prophet Isaiah, but they would remember that he walked naked and barefoot through the streets of Jerusalem (Isa. ch. 20), that he gave his children strange names, Shear-jashuv (a remnant will return, 7:3) and Maher-shalal-hashbaz (spoil hastens, booty hurries, 8:1). People might misunderstand or turn a deaf ear to what Jeremiah said or seek to silence him, but the odd things he did made them think, not least what he did here with a good linen waistcloth.

Some things are not wholly clear about this incident. It is not even certain what the linen waistcloth was. In other Old Testament passages the word translated "waistcloth" seems to refer to a belt or a girdle. Here it probably means a short skirt worn next to the skin under the long outer garment—underpants, if you like. In terms of the symbolism of the incident the important thing about it was that it was new, straight from the manufacturer, straight out of the cellophane wrapping. This new and hitherto unmarked article of clothing Jeremiah is told to take and hide in "a cleft of the rock" (verse 4). The effect would be just like burying your best shirt or slip in the back garden! But where did he hide it? Beside the Euphrates, say the traditional English translations. This would have involved Jeremiah in a round trip of seven hundred miles, and in a lengthy absence from home which might have well prompted people to ask, "Where have you been?" The Hebrew word translated Euphrates might equally well, however, refer to the small village of Perat, modern Ain Farah, a few miles north-east of Anathoth. This is how the NEB renders, and this is perhaps more likely.

Whatever the uncertainty in detail, the meaning of the incident is crystal clear and is spelled out in verse 9. The new linen cloth, left in the cleft of the rock for "many days", is retrieved by Jeremiah and found, naturally enough, to be spoiled. "Even so," says the Lord, "will I spoil the pride of Judah and the great pride of Jerusalem." Verses 10–11 then go on to explain the reason for this spoiling, that tragic contrast between the people as they have turned out to be, stubborn, unfaithful; and what they were intended to be, bound close to God and celebrating their relationship with him in the world. To substitute arrogance, based on false claims to privilege, for that humble obedience which is the mark of a true relationship with God, can only spell ruin.

Everything was grist to the prophet's mill as he sought to bring his people face to face with coming disaster. In verses 12–14 he fastens on a well-known saying or a popular proverb: "Every jar shall be filled with wine". To which the obvious retort is, tell us something new, that's what wine jars are for, isn't it? A good supply of wine guarantees a good party. The wine jars, however, were made of earthenware and were easily broken in the course of a drunken party, just as tumblers and wine glasses get smashed today. So there are two related themes in this passage:

(1) *Drunkenness*. There are passages in Jeremiah—and in other prophets—which speak of God handing either to Israel or to other nations the cup of the wine of his anger so that they may drink it till they fall in a drunken stupor (Jer. 25:15–17; Isa. 51:17)—a vivid way of talking about the reality of God's judgement. This may be the meaning here, or the passage may simply be saying that the entire community is drunk and incapable, incapable of acting in the way God requires.

(2) *The smashing of wine jars*. This leads naturally into the theme of the community irrevocably smashed by God. The theme is, therefore, similar to that of the spoiled waistcloth, so it is

hardly surprising that the two passages are placed side by side in the book of Jeremiah. We shall hear later of another incident in which Jeremiah deliberately smashes a jar to underline a similar message (see chapter 19).

FINAL WORDS OF WARNING

Jeremiah 13:15–27

15Hear and give ear; be not proud,
    for the Lord has spoken.
16Give glory to the Lord your God
    before he brings darkness,
before your feet stumble
    on the twilight mountains,
and while you look for light
    he turns it into gloom
    and makes it deep darkness.
17But if you will not listen,
    my soul will weep in secret for your pride;
my eyes will weep bitterly and run down with tears,
    because the Lord's flock has been taken captive.

18Say to the king and the queen mother:
    "Take a lowly seat,
for your beautiful crown
    has come down from your head."
19The cities of the Negeb are shut up,
    with none to open them;
all Judah is taken into exile,
    wholly taken into exile.

20"Lift up your eyes and see
    those who come from the north.
Where is the flock that was given you,
    your beautiful flock?
21What will you say when they set as head over you
    those whom you yourself have taught
    to be friends to you?
Will not pangs take hold of you,
    like those of a woman in travail?

²²And if you say in your heart,
   'Why have these things come upon me?'
 it is for the greatness of your iniquity
   that your skirts are lifted up,
   and you suffer violence.
²³Can the Ethiopian change his skin
   or the leopard his spots?
 Then also you can do good
   who are accustomed to do evil.
²⁴I will scatter you like chaff
   driven by the wind from the desert.
²⁵This is your lot,
   the portion I have measured out to you, says the Lord,
 because you have forgotten me
   and trusted in lies.
²⁶I myself will lift up your skirts over your face,
   and your shame will be seen.
²⁷I have seen your abominations,
   your adulteries and neighings, your lewd harlotries,
   on the hills in the field.
 Woe to you, O Jerusalem!
   How long will it be
   before you are made clean?"

There is a grim finality about this passage.

(1) In the first section, verses 15–17, the prophet seems to be appealing to the people to change, to strip themselves of their proud defiance of God. Yet there is no hint that he has any hope that they will. They may still be fondly expecting to see light at the end of the tunnel, but in fact they are stepping into the deadly gloom of murky darkness. The word translated "gloom" in verse 16 is the word traditionally translated in Ps. 23:4 as "the shadow of death", but which the NEB more correctly renders "dark as death" and the Good News Bible "deepest darkness". If the people are tempted to complain about their present plight, let them be warned; present difficulties are mere "twilight" compared with the impenetrable darkness to come. Amos uses similar language when he seeks to burst the bubble of popular religious complacency in his day (Amos 5:18–20). In the darkness

we hear again the tears of Jeremiah, tears because of what the people are, and tears because of the tragic fate that awaits them. This is true compassion and sympathy. Often these two things are separated; regret at the evil which ruins people's lives can sadly go hand in hand with delight at the prospect that they are going to get what they richly deserve.

(2) Verses 18–19 contain a lament addressed to the "king and the queen mother". The king is Jehoiachin who occupied the throne for a brief three months after the death in 597 B.C. of his father Jehoiakim who had rebelled against his Babylonian overlord. Jehoiachin was replaced on the throne by a Babylonian nominee and exiled to Babylon where he spent many long and in the end not wholly uncongenial years (52:31–34). He never returned to his homeland. To understand what such separation from the homeland could mean to a sensitive Jew read Psalm 137. The Queen Mother seems to have had an important role in the Jerusalem political establishment. 2 Kings 24:8 gives her name as Nehushta. Although the Negeb strictly speaking is the arid, semi-desert region which marks the southern boundary between Judah and Egypt, the "cities of the Negeb" referred to in verse 18 probably mean all the southern Judean towns under siege by the Babylonian invasion forces. Exile is the threat that hangs over the whole land.

(3) As the Greek translation of the text has rightly seen, Jerusalem is being addressed in verses 20ff., Jerusalem who, having flirted with the Babylonians to secure her own political future (verse 21), now finds these same "friends" dismembering her. But could it not have been otherwise? No, says Jeremiah, the evil in the nation's life is so deeply ingrained that it is indelible. You might as well ask an Ethiopian to change the colour of his dark skin or ask a leopard to get rid of its spots (verse 23).

There is a profoundly pessimistic note being sounded here. The Old Testament knows no doctrine of original sin. The story of the Garden of Eden was never so interpreted in the Old Testament or by later Jewish scholars. Jeremiah is giving no more than a realistic assessment of the Jerusalem of his day. Here was a community which would not, and apparently could not change.

Play with evil long enough and it takes over. The outcome can
only be total disaster for the nation. There is an element of poetic
justice in the language used to describe coming disaster. Just as
the attractive sexuality of the fertility cults had undermined the
people's loyalty to the Lord (verse 27), so their fate is described in
terms of rape and sexual dishonour. Twice we hear the words
"lifted up your skirts" (verses 22 and 26), and in verse 22 it is
followed by a phrase which could be literally translated "your
heels suffer violence", with the word "heels" probably being a
euphemism for the sexual organs. In verse 26 it is followed by the
phrase "your shame [i.e. your nakedness] will be seen".

The passage ends in a question, a question God asks of the
people. The meaning of the Hebrew text is unclear, and has led to
various interpretations. Does it mean "how much longer will this
go on?" or "how much longer will it be before you repent?"
Either way it is a question that only the people can answer. They
are being forced to face the fact that the problem lies not in their
stars, nor in God, but in themselves. It is only too easy for us to try
to blame God for the things that upset us or that we do not
understand. We want to put him in the witness-box. It is one way
of avoiding the awkward questions with which God is continually
facing us. If you look at the book of Job you will find Job asks a lot
of very awkward questions of God and demands answers. There
is nothing wrong in this; there are questions that we should be
asking. But the book comes to its climax with Job in the witness-
box, facing questions from God which challenge his whole attitude to life. So with Jesus; he does not seem to have left people
with many questions about God, but he did leave them facing a
lot of heart-searching questions about themselves.

A NATIONAL CRISIS

Jeremiah 14:1–16

[1]The word of the Lord which came to Jeremiah concerning the
drought:
[2]"Judah mourns

and her gates languish;
her people lament on the ground,
   and the cry of Jerusalem goes up.
³Her nobles send their servants for water;
   they come to the cisterns,
they find no water,
   they return with their vessels empty;
they are ashamed and confounded
   and cover their heads.
⁴Because of the ground which is dismayed,
   since there is no rain on the land,
the farmers are ashamed,
   they cover their heads.
⁵Even the hind in the field forsakes her newborn calf
   because there is no grass.
⁶The wild asses stand on the bare heights,
   they pant for air like jackals;
their eyes fail
   because there is no herbage.

⁷"Though our iniquities testify against us,
   act, O Lord, for thy name's sake;
for our backslidings are many,
   we have sinned against thee.
⁸O thou hope of Israel,
   its saviour in time of trouble,
why shouldst thou be like a stranger in the land,
   like a wayfarer who turns aside to tarry for a night?
⁹Why shouldst thou be like a man confused,
   like a mighty man who cannot save?
Yet thou, O Lord, art in the midst of us,
   and we are called by thy name;
   leave us not."

¹⁰Thus says the Lord concerning this people:
"They have loved to wander thus,
   they have not restrained their feet;
therefore the Lord does not accept them,
   now he will remember their iniquity
   and punish their sins."

11The Lord said to me: "Do not pray for the welfare of this people. 12Though they fast, I will not hear their cry, and though they offer burnt offering and cereal offering, I will not accept them; but I will consume them by the sword, by famine, and by pestilence."

13Then I said: "Ah, Lord God, behold, the prophets say to them, 'You shall not see the sword, nor shall you have famine, but I will give you assured peace in this place.'" 14And the Lord said to me: "The prophets are prophesying lies in my name; I did not send them, nor did I command them or speak to them. They are prophesying to you a lying vision, worthless divination, and the deceit of their own minds. 15Therefore thus says the Lord concerning the prophets who prophesy in my name although I did not send them, and who say, 'Sword and famine shall not come on this land': By sword and famine those prophets shall be consumed. 16And the people to whom they prophesy shall be cast out in the streets of Jerusalem, victims of famine and sword, with none to bury them—them, their wives, their sons, and their daughters. For I will pour out their wickedness upon them."

Every nation has its own state occasions on which it celebrates what it regards as important for its life, whether it be a May Day parade in Red Square, Independence Day, or a solemn service of Remembrance. These are always occasions hedged around with traditions. Certain things are said and done—for example the two minutes' silence on Remembrance Sunday—and as long as the community retains its identity everyone knows why this is the way such a day is celebrated. It was no different in ancient Israel. It had its great national day of remembrance, Passover, when the people remembered how the Lord had delivered them out of enslavement in Egypt to make them his people, and relived that experience. So it was in situations of grave national crisis, and on days that recalled such crises, the community would gather in the Temple courts at Jerusalem to share in what we call a community lament.

There are several very good examples of such community laments in the Psalms, among them Psalm 44 and Psalm 74. Such laments have certain common recurring features:

(i) they describe a situation of crisis in the life of the community—it may be military disaster, famine or drought

(ii) they give voice to the people's response to such a crisis, often through the puzzled, agonising questions "Why?" or "How long, O Lord?"

(iii) they very often end with an appeal to the God who has proved his power and grace in the past to do something to remedy the desperate present.

Drought was such a crisis situation in Old Testament times. It still is today for many people in the underdeveloped countries of the world, as we see only too tragically on our TV screens, the choking dust, the emaciated limbs and distended bellies of children dying of starvation. Chapter 14:1–9 is a community lament as the people find themselves in the relentless grip of a drought, vividly described in verses 1–6—the futile search for water, the farmers giving up the unequal struggle, the livestock and the wild animals with the glazed look of death in their eyes. Briefly the people confess their sins and urgently turn to the Lord. Why has he apparently deserted his people; why does he seem to be powerless to do anything to help them? They call upon him to prove once again that they are his people and that he is caringly in their midst (verses 7–9). In the midst of unanswered questions, they have nowhere to go but to God.

On such occasions of national lament a word of assurance was sometimes spoken to the people in God's name by a priest or Temple prophet (see Ps. 60:6–8). In verse 10 we hear such a word, but it is not a word of assurance; it is a word confirming God's rejection of the people. To hold out hope when there is no hope is the cruellest of mockeries. So this drought does not merely give rise to a community lament; it is an occasion when the word comes again to Jeremiah (14:1), confirming his message of judgement.

Now we must try honestly to face a difficulty here. We do not look at our world today and think of natural catastrophes like drought as the judgement of God upon a sinful people. Our immediate response is to see how help can be given through international agencies like the Red Cross or Christian Aid or Oxfam. Yet the Old Testament does think in these terms (see Amos 4:6–10 and the comments on Jer. 4:23–26). However much we may want to talk about the way in which our human existence is bound up with our natural environment, this is still miles away from the Old Testament attitude. We must accept that. But notice one thing. Jeremiah's message of judgement does not come out of the drought, nor is it the drought that convinces him of the corruption of the community. He finds in the drought confirmation of what he already believes for other reasons. The drought is a warning sign that ought to have made the people take a long hard look at themselves; and warnings ignored, as Amos 4:6ff. underline, bring tragic consequences.

THE TRUE AND THE FALSE WORD (verses 11–16)

To the community lament there has been appended a section in prose which picks up the sombre theme of judgement in verse 10 and uses it to stress once more the difference between the true and the false prophet. For the third time we hear the Lord say to Jeremiah, do not pray for this people (cf. 7:16; 11:14), certainly do not pray for their "welfare", their prosperity, their good (Hebrew *tovah*). The only thing they have to look forward to is the terrible triplets who accompanied war in the ancient world— sword, famine and plague. But, protests Jeremiah, there are prophets who are assuring the people that such calamities will not happen, that their future is one of enduring *shalom* (see comment on 6:14). In reply the Lord categorically denies that he has had anything to do with such prophets. They offer nothing but what comes out of their own warped minds; their visions are lies, their thoughts about the future worthless. This is an assessment of such prophets which we shall see more fully discussed in 23:9–40, and we shall return to it when we come to that passage.

Deceivers and liars—that is the verdict on such prophets. What else could they be to Jeremiah since the message they proclaimed was in direct conflict with what he had to say? Yet there comes a time when, as we shall see (20:7), Jeremiah himself begins to wonder whether he is not being deceived by the Lord. If even he had such a doubt, how much more difficult must it have been for the people to know that the true word of the Lord was on the lips of this lone dissenter, and not on the lips of the prophets who in the Lord's name said to them, "Sword and famine shall not come on this land" (verse 15). When the bodies of these prophets and of the people who believed them lie unburied in the streets of Jerusalem, then it will be seen that they were deceived. Only then it will be too late. If only they had known: but one of the ironies of life is that we seldom do know and that we often take the wrong choices for what we believe are the best of reasons, not least Christians who most loudly proclaim that they are led by the spirit of Christ.

A FURTHER LAMENT AND COMMENT

Jeremiah 14:17–15:4

17"You shall say to them this word:
'Let my eyes run down with tears night and day,
    and let them not cease,
for the virgin daughter of my people is smitten with a great wound,
    with a very grievous blow.
18If I go out into the field,
    behold, those slain by the sword!
And if I enter the city,
    behold, the diseases of famine!
For both prophet and priest ply their trade through the land,
    and have no knowledge.'"

19Hast thou utterly rejected Judah?
    Does thy soul loathe Zion?
Why hast thou smitten us
    so that there is no healing for us?
We looked for peace, but no good came;
    for a time of healing, but behold, terror.
20We acknowledge our wickedness, O Lord,
    and the iniquity of our fathers,
    for we have sinned against thee.
21Do not spurn us, for thy name's sake;
    do not dishonour thy glorious throne;
    remember and do not break thy covenant with us.

²²Are there any among the false gods of the nations that can bring
   rain?
   Or can the heavens give showers?
Art thou not he, O Lord our God?
   We set our hope on thee,
   for thou doest all these things.

¹Then the Lord said to me, "Though Moses and Samuel stood before
me, yet my heart would not turn toward this people. Send them out of
my sight, and let them go! ²And when they ask you, 'Where shall we
go?' you shall say to them, 'Thus says the Lord:
   "Those who are for pestilence, to pestilence,
      and those who are for the sword, to the sword;
   those who are for famine, to famine,
      and those who are for captivity, to captivity."'
³"I will appoint over them four kinds of destroyers, says the Lord: the
sword to slay, the dogs to tear, and the birds of the air and the beasts of
the earth to devour and destroy. ⁴And I will make them a horror to all
the kingdoms of the earth because of what Manasseh the son of
Hezekiah, king of Judah, did in Jerusalem."

Now we listen to a second lament, not this time related to
drought, but to military defeat and subsequent famine. It would
be a fitting response to the first Babylonian invasion and occupation of Jerusalem in 597 B.C. As elsewhere in the Old Testament
(e.g. Lam. ch. 3) this community lament has a section, verses
17–18, which uses the first person singular "I". Here someone—
in this case the prophet himself—identifies himself with the community and speaks on its behalf. Another section, verses 19–22,
uses the first person plural "we".

The description of the national crisis in verses 17–18 ends with a
comment on "prophet and priest" whose meaning is far from
certain. The RSV translation seems to imply that even now that
disaster has struck, prophet and priest still hawk their dubious
wares throughout the land. The NEB translation says of these
prophets and priests, now doubtless discredited, that they "go
begging round the land, and are never at rest", words which
might equally well be rendered "have roamed to a land they know
not", a reference to the fact that the religious leadership in the

community has been sent into exile. From the description of the crisis the lament moves into the urgent questions forced upon the people by the negation of all their fondest hopes. Has God rejected his people? Is this the end? Why did it happen? Why is there no light in the darkness?—all the questions we still ask when we are faced with crisis situations in our own life. Confession then gives way to an appeal to God to be true to his own purposes and character, to remember the bond (the covenant) which he made with Israel. This appeal is underlined by a moving affirmation of faith in the power of Israel's God (verse 22).

Just as the lament on the drought was capped by a prose passage in the form of a word from the Lord to Jeremiah, so is this lament. Nowhere is the Lord's rejection of the people more strongly stated than in the claim that even if Moses and Samuel prayed on behalf of the people it would make no difference. Moses and Samuel had quite a reputation as being men of effective prayer. Faced with the Lord's threat to wipe out a rebellious people, Moses, according to Exod. 32:11, prayed on their behalf and the Lord changed his mind (cf. Deut. 9:13ff.). Likewise, Samuel on several occasions successfully interceded with the Lord on behalf of the people (1 Sam. 7:8–9; 12:19–25).

But not now. Nothing can make God change his mind. When in their distress the people ask "Where shall we go?" (15:2), the answer is clear and grim—destination death (RSV "pestilence" in verse 2 is wrong), or the sword . . . or famine . . . or captivity. They are to become a terrifying example to others of the results of that record of national apostasy which King Manasseh had done so much to foster. King Manasseh had kept Judah at peace for most of the first half of the seventh century B.C. by faithfully licking the boots of his Assyrian imperial overlord. He bought security and peace at a price, the price of encouraging the worship of many gods, including Assyrian gods, in Jerusalem. This made him in the eyes of the historian in 2 Kings chapter 21 the archheretic, the symbol of all that sealed the fate of the people of God. It is always possible to buy peace at a price, often at the price of compromising on the very issues on which we know we ought to take a stand.

JERUSALEM LEFT TO HER FATE

Jeremiah 15:5–9

5"Who will have pity on you, O Jerusalem,
  or who will bemoan you?
 Who will turn aside
  to ask about your welfare?
6You have rejected me, says the Lord,
  you keep going backward;
 so I have stretched out my hand against you and destroyed you;—
  I am weary of relenting.
7I have winnowed them with a winnowing fork
  in the gates of the land;
 I have bereaved them, I have destroyed my people;
  they did not turn from their ways.
8I have made their widows more in number
  than the sand of the seas;
 I have brought against the mothers of young men
  a destroyer at noonday;
 I have made anguish and terror
  fall upon them suddenly.
9She who bore seven has languished;
  she has swooned away;
 her sun went down while it was yet day;
  she has been shamed and disgraced.
 And the rest of them I will give to the sword
  before their enemies,
            says the Lord."

This brief poem probably reflects the Babylonian capture of Jerusalem in 597 B.C., just as the book of Lamentations comes out of the aftermath of the more violent end of Jerusalem at the hands of the Babylonians a decade later. The stark reality of God's destruction of his own people is sketched in several arresting pictures.

(1) Farmers used to bring their harvested grain to a communal threshing floor, usually on a small mound outside the village. There the sheaves were chopped into pieces by a heavy wooden sledge being driven over them. The chopped grain was then

tossed into the air by a winnowing fork to allow the wind to blow away the chaff. So Israel had been winnowed by the Lord, blown away like chaff, presumably a reference to those who, at that time, had been deported to exile.

(2) Here is a community in deep grief, inhabited by widows whose menfolk had been slain in battle, and by mothers who would once have claimed to have been richly blessed by the Lord—seven sons were an ideal family (see Ruth 4:15)—but for whom now the light of life has been extinguished.

This is a community forsaken, because it has repeatedly forsaken God. There comes a time when even God can take no more (verse 6). The opening words of the poem provide a suitable epitaph:

> Who will have pity on you, O Jerusalem,
>> or who will bemoan you?
> Who will turn aside
>> to ask about your welfare? (verse 5)

This is a community which for long had hoped and prayed for *shalom*; now, ironically, there is no one left who will even bother to ask about such *shalom*. Even their false, deluding dreams are gone.

INNER STRUGGLES (i)

Jeremiah 15:10–21

[10]Woe is me, my mother, that you bore me, a man of strife and contention to the whole land! I have not lent, nor have I borrowed, yet all of them curse me. [11]So let it be, O Lord, if I have not entreated thee for their good, if I have not pleaded with thee on behalf of the enemy in the time of trouble and in the time of distress! [12]Can one break iron, iron from the north, and bronze?

[13]"Your wealth and your treasures I will give as spoil, without price, for all your sins, throughout all your territory. [14]I will make you serve your enemies in a land which you do not know, for in my anger a fire is kindled which shall burn for ever."

[15]O Lord, thou knowest;

remember me and visit me,
and take vengeance for me on my persecutors.
In thy forbearance take me not away;
know that for thy sake I bear reproach.
¹⁶Thy words were found, and I ate them,
and thy words became to me a joy
and the delight of my heart;
for I am called by thy name,
O Lord, God of hosts.
¹⁷I did not sit in the company of merrymakers,
nor did I rejoice;
I sat alone, because thy hand was upon me,
for thou hadst filled me with indignation.
¹⁸Why is my pain unceasing,
my wound incurable,
refusing to be healed?
Wilt thou be to me like a deceitful brook,
like waters that fail?

¹⁹Therefore thus says the Lord:
"If you return, I will restore you,
and you shall stand before me.
If you utter what is precious, and not what is worthless,
you shall be as my mouth.
They shall turn to you,
but you shall not turn to them.
²⁰And I will make you to this people
a fortified wall of bronze;
they will fight against you,
but they shall not prevail over you,
for I am with you
to save you and deliver you,
says the Lord.
²¹I will deliver you out of the land of the wicked,
and redeem you from the grasp of the ruthless."

We come back to the prophet and the inner tensions which threaten to tear him apart. But before we seek to understand the light which this section throws on the spiritual life of Jeremiah we must reckon with difficult problems in the text.

(1) Verses 13–14 occur again, in a much more natural setting, as part of chapter 17:3–4. If, however, we take verse 12 to be referring to the irresistible power of the enemy from the north who has sealed the fate of Jerusalem, then we can see why verses 13–14, which describe the despoiling of the people and coming exile, were considered appropriate in this context.

(2) Verse 11 has given rise to many interpretations and there can be little certainty as to its precise meaning. Who is speaking? The RSV, following the Greek text, assumes that it is Jeremiah, and that he is solemnly denying that he has done anything to deserve the hatred which he has aroused. Yet we might equally well be hearing a continuing cry of despair from Jeremiah, for we could translate the first half of the verse "Truly, Lord, I have not served you to any good effect". But is it Jeremiah who is speaking? If we are following the traditional Hebrew text the speaker is the Lord, the verse there beginning "The Lord said". This introduces what may well have been a word of reassurance, which the NEB renders:

> But I will greatly strengthen you;
>> in time of distress and in time of disaster
>> I will bring the enemy to your feet.

Beyond all the uncertainties of the text, however, certain things are clear. We have here two autobiographical passages separated by verses 13–14.

The first begins with a bitter cry of despair. Life, for Jeremiah, has become one long hassle. He is a marked man, continually at loggerheads with the rest of the community. All of which would have been fair enough if he had been a detested money-lender, exacting exorbitant interest from his fellow-citizens (Deut. 23:19) or if he had been defaulting on a loan; but he is on the receiving end of others' curses for no reason at all. Would it not have been better never to have been born? The same theme is expressed even more vigorously and dramatically in 20:14–18.

This is a very uncharacteristic mood in the Old Testament. Life is God's gift, God's good gift to be enjoyed to the full. Even the author of Psalm 22, in the dark night of his soul, draws comfort from the fact that it was God who gave him life, who took him from his mother's womb (Ps. 22:9). Only in Job, in a situation of extreme suffering where life seems to have lost all meaning, do we have any parallel to this cry of Jeremiah (Job ch. 3)—and Jeremiah's words may have influenced the author of Job. We dare not underestimate the dread reality of the despair which gripped the prophet. There were moments in his life when all seemed to be dark.

INNER STRUGGLES (ii)

Jeremiah 15:10–21 (*cont'd*)

The second passage, verses 15–21, has many of the marks of the personal laments which we find in the Psalms (see comment on 14:1–16). It begins with a plea for deliverance, a plea rooted in the conviction "O Lord, thou knowest" (verse 15), you, O God, if anyone, are aware of the situation I face, you know the depths of my despair, and since you know, you can do something. So act to "take vengeance for me on my persecutors", act to confirm me in my calling since all my difficulties are the result of that calling.

Here we find light being thrown on the cost of discipleship for Jeremiah. He claims in verse 16 to have gladly accepted his calling as the bearer of God's word to the people, and it is hard to see how any ministry can be sustained without such inner joy and commitment. The expression "Thy words were found, and I ate them" recalls the strange experience of Ezekiel who, according to Ezek. 2:9, was handed a written scroll and told to eat it. When he did, he found it to be "as sweet as honey". Whether Jeremiah did something equally strange or whether this is simply a pictorial way of saying "I have digested the message you gave me", we do not know. His, then, was a ministry gladly accepted, but there was a price to be paid. There was the cost of loneliness, a loneliness inevitably forced upon him by his prophetic calling. He was an outsider, obsessed by a sense of coming doom, unable to fit into the social round, its parties, its carefree enjoyment. There is no reason to assume that Jeremiah was naturally an anti-social type; indeed it is more likely that the words of verse 17 are the words of a sensitive man who longed to be accepted by others, but found acceptance denied to him because of his prophetic ministry. You will find similar sentiments on the lips of the Psalmist in Ps. 26:4–5, but in the more general context of the contrast between the righteous, to whom he claimed to belong, and the wicked whom he shuns.

As his fellow men shut the doors in his face, Jeremiah turns to God with a bitter complaint. Why must I endure this intolerable and unending tension? A nagging doubt crosses his mind:

> Wilt thou be to me like a deceitful brook,
> like waters that fail? (verse 18)

"A deceitful brook" refers to one of these Palestinian wadis or gorges that carry a great volume of water in the rainy season but are mockingly dry in the heat of the summer when the thirsty traveller is in most need of water. Yet Jeremiah had preached to his people faith in a God whom he had described, in contrast to all other gods, as a "fountain of living waters" (2:13). But what if this "fountain of living waters" turns out to be "a deceitful brook"? What if the message he had so confidently preached to others no longer makes sense in his own life? Can you continue to witness to others when your own faith dries up?

In reply the Lord gives Jeremiah a promise (verses 20–21), in essence a repetition of the promise that Jeremiah had heard at his call (see 1:8, 18–19), not, as we have seen, the promise of an easy passage, but the promise of God's presence to "save . . . deliver . . . and redeem", all of them words that point to release or escape from a difficult situation. Notice that this is no new promise. It has been well said that we far more often need to be reminded of truths we already know than to be taught new truths. It is as if God is saying to Jeremiah, "Instead of complaining that you don't have adequate resources, cash the cheque you have already been given".

There is, however, one very interesting thing about this promise. It is a conditional promise, and the condition is surprising:

If you return, I will restore you. (verse 19)

or more literally:

If you turn, I will cause you to turn.

Jeremiah's insistent message to the people had been "turn . . . turn back to God" (see the section 3:1–4:4), and he had spelled out for them the conditions of such a true turning. Now the message he had so confidently preached to others, he hears directed against himself . . . *you* turn. But why, and from what, did Jeremiah need to turn? We do not know. Is the answer to be found in the second half of verse 19?

If you utter what is precious, and not what is worthless,
  you shall be as my mouth.
They shall turn to you,
  but you shall not turn to them.

Is there an implied rebuke in these words? Is it possible that in the face of mounting opposition and indifference Jeremiah was tempted to trim his sails, to make his message a bit more palatable to his audience? There is no evidence of this in the book, but behind the outer uncompromising certainty of the words Jeremiah spoke in public, there may lie an inner struggle in which the temptation to compromise was only too real.

Or was it perhaps the very intensity of his religious commitment that was the problem? Had he set his feet on the path of Pharisaism, that occupational disease of the devout in every age? Had his very earnestness separated him from the people for whose sake the word had been given to him? Had he become more concerned for his own reputation than for the God whose servant he was called to be? We do not know, but this at least we do know; Jeremiah was being reminded that the world could not be divided into the one perfect saint, and the rest, miserable sinners. He was not himself exempt from the challenge of the message he preached to others.

NORMAL LIFE AT AN END

Jeremiah 16:1–13

¹The word of the Lord came to me: ²"You shall not take a wife, nor shall you have sons or daughters in this place. ³For thus says the Lord concerning the sons and daughters who are born in this place, and concerning the mothers who bore them and the fathers who begot them in this land: ⁴They shall die of deadly diseases. They shall not be lamented, nor shall they be buried; they shall be as dung on the surface of the ground. They shall perish by the sword and by famine, and their dead bodies shall be food for the birds of the air and for the beasts of the earth.

⁵"For thus says the Lord: Do not enter the house of mourning, or go to lament, or bemoan them; for I have taken away my peace from this people, says the Lord, my steadfast love and mercy. ⁶Both great and small shall die in this land; they shall not be buried, and no one shall lament for them or cut himself or make himself bald for them. ⁷No one shall break bread for the mourner, to comfort him for the dead; nor shall any one give him the cup of consolation to drink for his father or his mother. ⁸You shall not go into the house of feasting to sit with them, to eat and drink. ⁹For thus says the Lord of hosts, the God of Israel: Behold, I will make to cease from this place, before your eyes and in your days, the voice of mirth and the voice of gladness, the voice of the bridegroom and the voice of the bride.

¹⁰"And when you tell this people all these words, and they say to you, 'Why has the Lord pronounced all this great evil against us? What is our iniquity? What is the sin that we have committed against the Lord our God?' ¹¹then you shall say to them: 'Because your fathers have forsaken me, says the Lord, and have gone after other gods and have served and worshipped them, and have forsaken me and have not kept my law, ¹²and because you have done worse than your fathers, for behold, every one of you follows his stubborn evil will, refusing to listen to me; ¹³therefore I will hurl you out of this land into a land which neither you nor your fathers have known, and there you shall serve other gods day and night, for I will show you no favour.'"

This passage gives another glimpse into the life of Jeremiah and into the way in which episodes in his life became the means of communicating God's message to the people. Most of our

English versions print verses 1–9 of chapter 16 as prose. They might equally well be treated as rough poetry, a mosaic of brief sayings in which the Lord addresses Jeremiah (verses 2, 5, 8), and speaks about the coming fate of the people (verses 3–4, 6–7, 9). It falls into three sections.

(1) *Marriage forbidden* (verses 1–4). We only get the full flavour of the words "You shall not take a wife, nor shall you have sons or daughters" (verse 2) when we realise that the bachelor bold was an unknown figure in ancient Israel. Marriage in normal circumstances was not optional. It was a family matter, and usually arranged at a fairly early age. Only through marriage was there the hope of the family name living on across the years. Celibacy was not an ideal, it was an abnormality. Jeremiah's celibacy, therefore, marked him off from other people. It was as unusual as Ezekiel's conduct on the death of his beloved wife (Ezek. 24:15ff.). At God's command Ezekiel broke all the social conventions associated with mourning. He got the inevitable response from other people, "Will you not tell us what these things mean for us, that you are acting thus?" (Ezek. 24:19). Out of his strange behaviour and the questions it provoked came the opportunity to declare God's word to the community. Jeremiah's celibacy also spoke. It was a dramatic way of saying to the people that normal life was coming to an end; there was no future for the community. Disaster was coming, disaster so shattering that the normal conventions of society no longer applied, not even the customary burial rites (verse 4).

Jeremiah renounced marriage in obedience to God, but there is always a price to be paid for such obedience. Being starved of normal human affection must have been one element in that desperate sense of loneliness which we noted in 15:17. Perhaps it was one of the psychological reasons for the bitter, almost savage cries for vengeance on his enemies which climax in 18:19–23.

(2) *Mourning forbidden* (verses 5–7). Mourning implies some degree of sympathy, some sense of belonging to the grieving family or the community of which it is a part. But this is a community which no longer has any links with God. He has withdrawn from it his peace (*shalom*), his steadfast love (*hesed*)

and his compassion. As God has broken his links with the people, so must his prophet. When Jeremiah absented himself from family or village mourning, at which he would normally have been expected to be present, this would again prompt the question "Why?" The prophet can only reply that any sharing of personal grief, by going to a house where mourners gather, is irrelevant, overshadowed by the stark reality of coming national tragedy so all-embracing and severe that the normal mourning customs can no longer be observed.

The habit of the mourner to "cut himself or make himself bald" (verse 6) refers to practices of gashing the flesh with knives and shaving the head, practices which are rigorously forbidden in the law (Lev. 19:28; Deut. 14:1)—doubtless because of their pagan associations—but which nevertheless seem to have been widely popular in ancient Israel. The reference in verse 7 to "bread for the mourner" and "the cup of consolation" probably refers to the food provided by neighbours for the family at the end of a mourning period of fasting. When a society dies, it is implied, the conventions through which it expresses its traditions and beliefs and round which it organises its life, die with it.

(3) *Festivity forbidden* (verses 8–9). As the context makes clear "the house of feasting" in verse 8 refers to a wedding party. If mourning is forbidden, so is its opposite, the laughter and the joy of the wedding festivities. When Jeremiah's absence from a family wedding was noted and commented on, he could only reply that a time was coming, and coming soon, when the sound of all wedding festivities would be silenced.

Jeremiah the celibate, conspicuously absent from family funerals and weddings alike—what a powerful, costly witness he made to the coming breakdown of all normal life in a God-forsaken community!

To this section there has been added in verses 10–13 a passage similar to 9:12–16 (see comment there) which:

   (i) asks a question; why is this disaster going to come?

  (ii) answers the question in terms of the nation's continuing apostasy; and

(iii) confirms the coming judgement, ironically commenting that the people will soon be off into exile, to distant, strange lands, where they can worship other gods to their hearts' content. In the light of their past record that should satisfy them!

LIGHT IN THE MIDST OF DARKNESS

Jeremiah 16:14–21

[14]"Therefore, behold, the days are coming, says the Lord, when it shall no longer be said, 'As the Lord lives who brought up the people of Israel out of the land of Egypt,' [15]but 'As the Lord lives who brought up the people of Israel out of the north country and out of all the countries where he had driven them.' For I will bring them back to their own land which I gave to their fathers.

[16]"Behold, I am sending for many fishers, says the Lord, and they shall catch them; and afterwards I will send for many hunters, and they shall hunt them from every mountain and every hill, and out of the clefts of the rocks. [17]For my eyes are upon all their ways; they are not hid from me, nor is their iniquity concealed from my eyes. [18]And I will doubly recompense their iniquity and their sin, because they have polluted my land with the carcasses of their detestable idols, and have filled my inheritance with their abominations."

[19]O Lord, my strength and my stronghold,
my refuge in the day of trouble,
to thee shall the nations come
from the ends of the earth and say:
"Our fathers have inherited naught but lies,
worthless things in which there is no profit.
[20]Can man make for himself gods?
Such are no gods!"

[21]"Therefore, behold, I will make them know, this once I will make them know my power and my might, and they shall know that my name is the Lord."

Nowhere are the problems of the book of Jeremiah better illustrated than in the section which begins at 16:14 and continues to 17:18. It is a very mixed bag, some of it poetry, some of it prose, and the relationship between the various bits and pieces is far from clear. It is almost as if an editor had picked up a pack of Jeremianic cards, shuffled them, and dealt them out at random. Since, however, there are a limited number of basic themes in the preaching of Jeremiah, the cards in our hand can be rearranged and put into appropriate suits.

We begin with three brief passages, (1) verses 14–15, (2) verses 16–18, and (3) verses 19–21. They are not obviously related to one another. If they contain authentic sayings of Jeremiah—and this has been seriously questioned—then they were probably spoken on different occasions and to different audiences in the course of his ministry.

(1) The first passage, verses 14–15, appears again in the book of Jeremiah at 23:7–8, in a much more natural setting, as one of a series of sayings whose common theme is hope for the future (23:1–8). It speaks of a new Exodus, of a coming day when the people will no longer merely confess their faith in "the Lord . . . who brought up the people of Israel out of the land of Egypt" (verse 14), at the beginning of Israel's history; but also in the Lord who brought his scattered people back from exile to their homeland. These words seem to have been placed here to balance the awesome severity of the previous section which ended in the threat of exile. The threatening words of verse 13, "I will hurl you out of this land into a land which neither you nor your fathers have known," are echoed in the hopeful words of verse 15, "I will bring them back to their own land which I gave to their fathers".

Do these words presuppose that the people are already in exile in Babylon? Certainly the theme of a new Exodus, a new beginning for God's people, is a common one in the teaching of the anonymous prophet of the Exile, whose message is to be found in Isaiah chapters 40–55. To exiles, wondering whether God still cared for them, these words would be particularly meaningful. Yet a message of hope in and beyond disaster is central to Jeremiah's own teaching. For more than a century, the people of the northern kingdom of Israel had been scattered to the far corners of the Assyrian empire, and the threat of exile for the people of Judah and Jerusalem loomed ever larger in Jeremiah's lifetime. False hopes based on illusory security Jeremiah vigorously attacked, but genuine hope, based on the conviction that the death of the nation, as he knew it, could not be the end of God's purposes for his people, remained to be nurtured. Perhaps we have here an example of such nurturing.

(2) The second passage, verses 16–18, returns to the theme of judgement. To illustrate it Jeremiah draws—as Jesus did and as every good preacher does—on the everyday life his people knew so well. There are the fishermen casting their nets for a catch. The prophet Habakkuk, a contemporary of Jeremiah, speaks of God having made men like fish of the sea, and says of the Babylonian invader:

> He brings all of them up with a hook,
> he drags them out with his net. (Hab. 1:15)

There too is the hunter relentlessly stalking his prey across the wildest terrain. From neither of them is there any escape; no more is there from the coming judgement of God (cf. Amos 9:1–4). Judgement is coming, and it is richly deserved. The words "I will doubly recompense their iniquity and their sin" should not be taken to mean that God is exacting an excess penalty. In certain legal cases, involving breach of trust, the appropriate penalty, according to the Old Testament law, was two-fold restitution (see Exod. 22:7–8). The people are in breach of trust. The land was the Lord's gift to them, but instead of caring for it they had "polluted" or defiled it with a multitude of idolatrous practices which Jeremiah sarcastically compares to corrupting corpses (cf. Lev. 26:30).

(3) The third passage, verses 19–21, speaks of a wider vision and a greater hope than the first; not merely the return of the people of Israel to their homeland, but the conversion of the nations who will renounce their false religions, their useless manmade gods, and turn to the one true God, the Lord who alone controls the destiny of all men. For this wider vision, which had often to struggle against a mood of religious nationalism and exclusiveness in Israel, see the comments on 4:2 and 12:14–17.

These three passages, awkwardly placed side by side, nevertheless highlight much that is central to Jeremiah's faith, and should be central to ours. There is the reality of the darkness, the seriousness with which God takes our human folly and sinfulness, and the mess we make of our world. But in and beyond the darkness there is light, the light of a hope rooted in the presence of a God whose purposes no evil of ours can finally destroy. A Jewish survivor of Auschwitz describes the day when the SS publicly executed three of his fellow Jews, two of them adults, one a young boy:

> Three necks were placed at the same moment within the nooses. "Long live liberty!" cried the adults. But the child was silent. "Where is God? Where is he?" someone behind me asked. . . . I heard a voice within me answer, "Where is God? Here he is—he is hanging on the gallows."

Darkness—there was no darker place than Auschwitz! Yet in the darkness there was light, the light of faith in God. If we know that light, we must remember it is not given for our own private comfort and illumination; it is a light meant for all men, a light given to be shared. In New Testament terms there is the cross and the cry of dereliction; there is the resurrection; there is a gospel for all the world!

THE INDELIBLE MARK OF SIN

Jeremiah 17:1–4

¹"The sin of Judah is written with a pen of iron; with a point of diamond it is engraved on the tablet of their heart, and on the horns of their altars, ²while their children remember their altars and their Asherim, beside every green tree, and on the high hills, ³on the mountains in the open country. Your wealth and all your treasures I will give for spoil as the price of your sin throughout all your territory. ⁴You shall loosen your hand from your heritage which I gave to you, and I will make you serve your enemies in a land which you do not know, for in my anger a fire is kindled which shall burn for ever."

While the people treated what was going on in the community with almost casual indifference, Jeremiah knew that there were no easy answers. The "sin of Judah", he says, is engraved on the heart, the conscience, the mind of the people, like an inscription chiselled into a rock face by an iron tool or a diamond point. There is no way in which it can be rubbed out or ignored. It is the need to deal with this hard fact of experience which leads on to the passage in 31:31–34. It talks about a new covenant, God-given, which will close the gap between what God requires and what the people give, by putting God's law within them, writing it on their hearts. It is the claim of the New Testament that this is precisely what happened in Jesus. In him we see the gap between God and man closed (see Heb. 8:6–13; 10:11–18).

No doubt the people would have admitted that they were not perfect, that mistakes were made, but could this not be dealt with by a good dose of religion? No, claims Jeremiah, your religion is the root of your problem. The sin of Judah is also engraved on "the horns of their altars". The horns of the altar projected upwards from the four corners on the top of the altar. They were made of stone, and carved into a horn shape. Whenever sacrifice was offered to God to deal with the sins of the people, some of the blood of the animal sacrificed was smeared on the horns of the altar (Lev. 4:7). It is clear from the ritual of the great Day of Atonement, as described in Leviticus chapter 16, that this was intended to ensure that the altar itself was cleansed from any contagion it might have received from the uncleanness of the people. But a little blood can cleanse neither the people nor their most sacred religious objects. There is plenty religion around; they have given their devotion to the fertility gods and goddesses (for the Asherim, verse 2, see comment on 2:27); they will reap a bitter harvest of national humiliation and exile. Verses 3–4 are similar to 15:13–14, but they have an additional sentence which underlines the tragedy of coming exile, a sentence which by a slight alteration to the traditional text may be rendered "you will lose your hold on the inheritance I gave to you".

THE CHOICE—TRUST IN MAN OR TRUST IN GOD

Jeremiah 17:5–8

> [5]Thus says the Lord:
> "Cursed is the man who trusts in man
>   and makes flesh his arm,
>   whose heart turns away from the Lord.
> [6]He is like a shrub in the desert,
>   and shall not see any good come.
> He shall dwell in the parched places of the wilderness,
>   in an uninhabited salt land.
>
> [7]"Blessed is the man who trusts in the Lord,
>   whose trust is the Lord.
> [8]He is like a tree planted by water,
>   that sends out its roots by the stream,
> and does not fear when heat comes,
>   for its leaves remain green,
> and is not anxious in the year of drought,
>   for it does not cease to bear fruit."

Read Psalm 1; notice the contrasting pictures it draws of the righteous man who prospers and the wicked man who perishes, and you will see why this passage is often thought to be little more than a variation on that Psalm. Since moreover, as we have seen (12:1–4), Jeremiah learned through bitter experience that life does not follow this script, it is hardly surprising that many scholars argue that this passage does not come from Jeremiah. But the links with Psalm 1 are not as close as are sometimes claimed. The contrast here is not between the wicked and the righteous, but between "the man who trusts in man" (verse 5) and "the man who trusts in the Lord" (verse 7).

We might approach this passage, then, as a further extract from Jeremiah's spiritual diary. Does this represent the prophet's response to God's call to him to "turn" in 15:19–21? Were the doubts and the dark moods of depression which had almost overwhelmed him rooted in the fact that he had begun to "trust in man" rather than in the Lord? Perhaps by trying to go it alone or by paying too much attention to what other people were saying, his faith in the Lord was weakening. It is hard to plough a lonely furrow, to hold on to what you believe, when everyone else is saying that you are wrong.

There is one snag in this, however. In similar passages Jeremiah is not usually so coy about saying that he is describing his own experience. When he means "I", he says "I", not "the man who...". It is better to take this passage as part of Jeremiah's preaching, an attack on those within the community who believed that Judah could only survive by successfully playing the game of power politics, by playing off the Egyptians against the Babylonians just as some countries today dabble in playing off Russia against the USA in bidding for military and economic aid. In a similar situation of political intrigue a hundred years earlier the prophet Isaiah rounds on those who go down to Egypt for aid, pointing out that

The Egyptians are men, and not God,
and their horses are flesh, and not spirit. (Isa. 31:3)

Isaiah calls upon his people to believe in the Lord's ability to protect Jerusalem. So here Jeremiah calls down a curse upon "the man who trusts in man and makes flesh his arm", and points his people to that which alone can survive when the heat is on and every prospect seems bleak, "trust in the Lord".

This message would have been peculiarly relevant in the aftermath of the reformation of 621 B.C. when so many hopes centred on the young Josiah, national hero, reforming king. Perhaps indeed this passage was prompted by the shock produced by the tragic death of Josiah at the battle of Megiddo in 609 B.C. For Judah nationalism, however much it claimed the blessing of religion, was not enough. To place your trust in man or in any kind of human power is ultimately a recipe for disillusionment. At no time in human history more than the present has there been such an urgent need to question putting trust in man. The human power is there, awesomely there, but to trust it is to invite the disillusionment of a nuclear holocaust.

FOLLY AND HOPE

Jeremiah 17:9–13

> ⁹The heart is deceitful above all things,
>   and desperately corrupt;
>   who can understand it?
> ¹⁰"I the Lord search the mind
>   and try the heart,
>   to give to every man according to his ways,
>   according to the fruit of his doings."
>
> ¹¹Like the partridge that gathers a brood which she did not hatch,
>   so is he who gets riches but not by right;
>   in the midst of his days they will leave him,
>   and at his end he will be a fool.
>
> ¹²A glorious throne set on high from the beginning
>   is the place of our sanctuary.
> ¹³O Lord, the hope of Israel,
>   all who forsake thee shall be put to shame;
>   those who turn away from thee shall be written in the earth,
>   for they have forsaken the Lord, the fountain of living water.

Verses 9–10 contain reflections on the mysterious perversity of the human mind. These verses have probably been placed here because they pick up certain key words from the previous passage, for example "heart" and "fruit". Verse 9 reads in Hebrew like one of those brief proverbial sayings, such as we find in the book of Proverbs. Experience teaches—it certainly taught Jeremiah—that the human mind (Hebrew "heart") can be strangely puzzling, often devious in the extreme. The human race can produce a St Francis and a Hitler, a Gandhi and a Stalin. Our motives for doing things are often hard to understand, even to those closest to us in life. Does anyone really know what goes on in the human mind? Only God, claims verse 10: "I the Lord search the mind and try the heart". The word translated "mind" in the first half of this verse, is the same word translated "heart" (Hebrew *lev*) in verse 9, while the word translated "heart" is the Hebrew word for "kidneys", the kidneys often being thought of as the seat of the emotions in Hebrew psychology. The two words are probably used here together to indicate the whole range of a man's inner life. And the Lord, who explores and tests this hidden inner life, rewards a man according to his deeds (see comment on 12:1–4).

There follows in verse 11 another proverb, which like many traditional proverbs, draws upon keen observation of what goes on in the world of nature. Thus Prov. 6:6:

> Go to the ant, O sluggard;
>   consider her ways, and be wise.

Compare Prov. 30:24–31. Consider, says Jeremiah, the partridge or the grouse. It was believed to hatch out eggs which it had not laid. Once hatched, the young birds soon realise that they do not belong to this strange mother bird, and quickly fly away. So is it, says the proverb, with riches unjustly acquired: quickly gotten and soon gone. The verdict on such a man who tries to get rich quick, and has few scruples as to how he gets there, can only be— he is a "fool", a man who has no clue as to what life is really all about. This proverb may be taken as one illustration of the truth that God deals with man according to his deeds.

Alongside this picture of human deviousness and folly, there has been placed a picture of the Lord as the sole hope of Israel, with a solemn warning to those who forsake him. The Temple in Jerusalem, referred to here as "our sanctuary", is described as "a glorious throne". This is the language of worship. In Ps. 132:13 the Temple is described as the place ". . . the Lord has chosen . . . he has desired it for his habitation". This is where the Lord dwells "enthroned upon the cherubim" (Ps. 80:1). The divine King is in the midst of his people.

Although in the Temple Sermon in chapter 7 Jeremiah bitingly attacks the false conclusions, the illusory security, that gripped the minds of the people when they thought of the presence of the Lord in their midst, in the Temple, there is no reason to assume that he doubted that the Temple was God's dwelling-place, and that there he was present with his truly worshipping people.

Because people draw false conclusions from certain ideas, not least religious ideas, that does not mean that they are wrong. The Lord *was* present, majestically present with his people, and this alone gave them solid ground for hope. To desert this God was to commit national and spiritual suicide. It is not clear what is meant by the words in verse 13 "those who turn away from thee *shall be written in the earth*". It makes more sense to alter the Hebrew text and either follow the NEB in translating the closing words "shall be humbled", or render "shall be cut off from the land". Once again we are being reminded that at the heart of worship, as at the heart of life, there are choices, choices which we are free to make; and with the consequences of our choices we must live.

A CRY FOR HELP

Jeremiah 17:14–18

> 14Heal me, O Lord, and I shall be healed;
> save me, and I shall be saved;
> for thou art my praise.
> 15Behold, they say to me,
> "Where is the word of the Lord?
> Let it come!"
> 16I have not pressed thee to send evil,
> nor have I desired the day of disaster,
> thou knowest;
> that which came out of my lips
> was before thy face.
> 17Be not a terror to me;
> thou art my refuge in the day of evil.
> 18Let those be put to shame who persecute me,
> but let me not be put to shame;
> let them be dismayed,
> but let me not be dismayed;
> bring upon them the day of evil;
> destroy them with double destruction!

This is an authentic *cri de coeur* from Jeremiah in the form of a lament. It begins with an urgent plea, a plea for healing and deliverance, a plea which has as its background that "pain unceasing" and "wound incurable" of which the prophet complains in 15:18. It is a plea which is possible because deep underneath the storms there is the swell of continuing confidence in God as the object of praise. This is a feature of many of the Psalms of lament, for example Psalms 4, 7, and 13. It is striking how in these autobiographical passages we find Jeremiah swinging between quiet confidence and agonising doubt. Both were real, both were part of his spiritual experience, as both are for many people today. Bishop Berggrav of Norway, describing his experience during the Nazi occupation of his country, speaks of half of his soul being in a hell of anxiety, fear and doubt, but the other half being carried on the wings of God-given faith.

The particular problem with which Jeremiah is wrestling in this passage is that most effective demoraliser—ridicule. If he began his ministry in 627 B.C. with a word of coming doom, then for many a long year nothing had happened except that there was a growing mood of self-confidence and security in Jerusalem. No wonder people mockingly said to him: "Where is the word of the Lord? Let it come!" (verse 15). Many may have concluded that Jeremiah was a classic example of a false prophet. How do you know a false prophet? One of the tests laid down in the book of Deuteronomy says: "When a prophet speaks in the name of the Lord, if the word does not come to pass or come true, that is a word which the Lord has not spoken; the prophet has spoken it presumptuously, you need not be afraid of him" (Deut. 18:22). "A discredited old scaremonger, at it again"—that was no doubt a popular response to Jeremiah's continuing preaching. It is hard to take ridicule.

So Jeremiah turns to the Lord with a complaint. He protests that he had taken no personal satisfaction out of preaching judgement. He had not sadistically wished disaster upon his people. All that he had done was to be faithful to the message God had given him. No doubt behind the complaint there is the thought that life would have been so much easier if only he had had a more acceptable message to preach. Complaint leads into a request, a two-fold request:

(1) that the Lord should stop hounding him, that instead of being a source of terror to him, he should be his "refuge", a word which is used over and over again in the Psalms to describe God (e.g. Pss. 11:1; 16:1; 46:1), a word which points to God as a source of the help, strength, and protection, which were not always part of Jeremiah's experience;

(2) that the terror which he had so often experienced, should be the lot of his persecutors. The word which the RSV translates "dismayed" in verse 18 comes from the same root as the word "terror" in verse 17. The NEB gets the flavour of this better by translating in verse 18, "may they be terrified, not I". Thus the passage ends in a raw cry for vengeance.

This time we only hear the prophet. There is no answering word from the Lord, no word of assurance (contrast 11:18ff. and 15:15–21). Perhaps it is reasonable to assume from this—as it is certainly true to our own experience—that there were times in Jeremiah's life when he prayed and there were no answers, when he sought help and had to go on struggling in the darkness, not seeing any light at the end of the tunnel.

A SERMON ON SABBATH OBSERVANCE

Jeremiah 17:19–27

¹⁹Thus said the Lord to me: "Go and stand in the Benjamin Gate, by which the kings of Judah enter and by which they go out, and in all the gates of Jerusalem, ²⁰and say: 'Hear the word of the Lord, you kings of Judah, and all Judah, and all the inhabitants of Jerusalem, who enter by these gates. ²¹Thus says the Lord: Take heed for the sake of your lives, and do not bear a burden on the sabbath day or bring it in by the gates of Jerusalem. ²²And do not carry a burden out of your houses on the sabbath or do any work, but keep the sabbath day holy, as I commanded your fathers. ²³Yet they did not listen or incline their ear, but stiffened their neck, that they might not hear and receive instruction.

²⁴"But if you listen to me, says the Lord, and bring in no burden by the gates of this city on the sabbath day, but keep the sabbath day holy and do no work on it, ²⁵then there shall enter by the gates of this city

kings who sit on the throne of David, riding in chariots and on horses, they and their princes, the men of Judah and the inhabitants of Jerusalem; and this city shall be inhabited for ever. [26]And people shall come from the cities of Judah and the places round about Jerusalem, from the land of Benjamin, from the Shephelah, from the hill country, and from the Negeb, bringing burnt offerings and sacrifices, cereal offerings and frankincense, and bringing thank offerings to the house of the Lord. [27]But if you do not listen to me, to keep the sabbath day holy, and not to bear a burden and enter by the gates of Jerusalem on the sabbath day, then I will kindle a fire in its gates, and it shall devour the palaces of Jerusalem and shall not be quenched.'"

Here is another of these sermons which may well go back to an element in Jeremiah's preaching, but which have probably been expanded and put into their present form during the Exile in Babylon. It contains the following:

(1) *An introduction* which sets the scene for the sermon. "Go and stand in the Benjamin Gate" (verse 19). The text which has been handed down to us, however, speaks not of "the Benjamin Gate", but "the gate of the sons of the people", which we might translate as "the People's Gate". No such gate as "the People's Gate", however, is known to us. If we change the text to "the Benjamin Gate", as do most translations, the scene is a gate in the north wall of the city of Jerusalem (cf. 37:13; 38:7). The further reference to "all the gates of Jerusalem" suggests that here is a sermon which the whole population of the city, from the least unto the greatest, must hear.

(2) *The preacher's theme* is the need to adhere strictly to one of the commandments of the law: "keep the sabbath day holy" (verse 22; see Exod. 20:8; Deut. 5:12). The urgency of the message is underlined by the opening words, which the RSV renders "Take heed for the sake of your lives" (verse 21), i.e. seriously consider what you are doing (see the similar phrase in Deut. 4:15); not least because the example of past generations is not exactly encouraging.

(3) *The congregation's choice*: the future lies in their own hands. Strict obedience to the demand for observance of the sabbath will lead to a prosperous future, to a secure and indepen-

dent state with its own royal family and court, with its capital city Jerusalem the religious centre of the nation's life. To it people will flock with their offerings from the land of Benjamin to the north, from the Shephelah, the rolling foothills to the west, from the hill country to the east, and from the Negeb in the south. Failure to keep the sabbath, however, will lead to national disaster (verse 27).

Other sermons in the book of Jeremiah, for example 11:1–8, ask for obedience to the total demands of the covenant relationship, but why this concentration on one commandment, and why the sabbath, the seventh day of the week as a day of rest? The origin of the sabbath is lost in the mists of Israel's early life, but the demand to keep it is there in the Ten Commandments, even if the versions of the Ten Commandments which we find in Exodus chapter 20 and Deuteronomy chapter 5 suggest different reasons for keeping it. It was widely observed in Israel before the Exile, and Jeremiah might well have had some sharp things to say about the failure of the community to observe it.

There is little doubt, however, that the sabbath became of increasing importance in Jewish life during and after the Exile and that it is to that age that this passage is speaking. The reason is simple. With the destruction of Jerusalem and its Temple, and the loss of national independence, much that had hitherto been regarded as central to Israel's religious life had been wiped out. But the sabbath needed no temple for its observance. By "the rivers of Babylon" (Ps. 137:1) or in any other place where fate or national tragedy had taken them, Jews could gather on the sabbath to remember the tradition of faith in which they had been nurtured, to listen to the words of the law. The observance of sabbath became one of the ways in which the increasingly scattered Jewish community could retain its identity as the people of God.

But the more important something becomes in the religious life of a people, the greater the danger that it will be misunderstood or misused. Just as Jeremiah had to demolish a false view of the Temple, so Jesus had some harsh things to say about the way in which the innumerable regulations which grew up around that particular institution were blinding people to the way in which the sabbath was there to help people to celebrate their faith (Mark 3:1–6; Matt. 12:1–14). Sadly the Christian Sunday, the first day of the week, the day which celebrates the resurrection triumph of Jesus, has suffered in certain Christian circles the same distortion. The note of celebration of the mighty acts of God has been lost in a harsh, negative piety, exactly the kind of piety which Jeremiah is so often at such pains to condemn.

IN THE POTTER'S WORKSHOP

Jeremiah 18:1–12

[1]The word that came to Jeremiah from the Lord: [2]"Arise, and go down to the potter's house, and there I will let you hear my words." [3]So I went down to the potter's house, and there he was working at his wheel. [4]And the vessel he was making of clay was spoiled in the potter's hand, and he reworked it into another vessel, as it seemed good to the potter to do.

[5]Then the word of the Lord came to me: [6]"O house of Israel, can I not do with you as this potter has done? says the Lord. Behold, like the clay in the potter's hand, so are you in my hand, O house of Israel. [7]If at any time I declare concerning a nation or a kingdom, that I will pluck up and break down and destroy it, [8]and if that nation, concerning which I have spoken, turns from its evil, I will repent of the evil that I intended to do to it. [9]And if at any time I declare concerning a nation or a kingdom that I will build and plant it, [10]and if it does evil in my sight, not listening to my voice, then I will repent of the good which I had intended to do to it. [11]Now, therefore, say to the men of Judah and the inhabitants of Jerusalem: 'Thus says the Lord, Behold, I am shaping evil against you and devising a plan against you. Return, every one from his evil way, and amend your ways and your doings.'

[12]"But they say, 'That is in vain! We will follow our own plans, and will every one act according to the stubbornness of his evil heart.'"

The potter's workshop was a familiar feature of life in the ancient world. The skills of the potter were always in demand. Pottery was in everyday use in the home, and was fragile. The modern archaeologist has ample reason to be grateful for the innumerable pieces of broken pottery which help him to build up a picture of life in ancient cities. In his workshop the potter would sit, spinning with his feet a large circular stone which rotated round a vertical axis. On top was another smaller stone, on which was placed the clay which took shape under the potter's skilled hands. That is why the word translated "wheel" in verse 3 is literally "two stones". Once shaped to the potter's liking on the wheel, the clay was glazed and baked in a furnace. You will find a thumbnail sketch of the potter at work in the book of Ecclesiasticus (Sirach) 38:29–30.

Jeremiah must often have stopped to look in at the village potter busy at his wheel. It was there in the workshop, as the potter was busy at his daily work, that the word of the Lord came to the prophet (see comment on 1:11–14). The clay was on the wheel, but the end result was not always acceptable to the potter. Perhaps the clay had not been quite the right consistency, perhaps the shape was not entirely to his liking. Sometimes the potter had to begin all over again, reshaping the clay, doing to the clay "as it seemed good to the potter to do" (verse 4). The word came to Jeremiah: here was a parable of God and Israel—God was the potter, Israel the clay: "Behold, like the clay in the potter's hand, so are you in my hand, O house of Israel" (verse 6).

But what does this mean? It has sometimes been claimed that this is essentially a message of hope: the clay, spoiled on the wheel, is reshaped by the potter till it comes up to his expectations. So Israel, flawed and misshapen, will continue to be reshaped by God until she truly reflects his purposes. But if that is so, then verses 7–12 are no part of the original incident, since they take a very different line. It has also been suggested that the incident turns on the quality of the clay. It is this which determines what the potter can do with it. So is it the quality of the people that determines what God can do with them. What God does to Israel, or to any nation, depends on how that nation responds or fails to respond in its life to what God demands. This view fits in better with verses 7–12, but it is not at all obvious that central to the incident is the quality of the clay.

The key issue is surely underlined in verse 4: it is the relationship between the potter and the clay. The clay is wholly under the control of the potter. He can do with it exactly what he likes. So is it with Israel, like clay in God's hands, totally under his control, at his disposal. God is free to do what he likes with his people. This could be a message of hope, but it could also be a message of judgement. It is underlining that Israel exists to serve God, not God to serve Israel. Israel can no more use God for her own purposes than the clay can dictate to the potter. You will find the picture of the potter and the clay used to make the same point in Isa. 45:9ff. (see also the comment on 2:19). There are times when people speak so glibly and confidently about God, and seem so certain that God will act in a way that will confirm their own religious prejudices, that one is tempted to say, "Go with Jeremiah to the potter's workshop".

This freedom of God is applied in verses 7–10 to his dealings with *any* nation or kingdom. It is a freedom which enables God to "repent", to change his mind, in the light of how people respond to him. A nation under sentence of death may be reprieved if it "turns from its evil" (verse 8), a nation basking in God's favour may be destroyed "if it does evil" (verse 10). The implications of this universal truth are then hammered home to God's own people Israel. They are under sentence by God. There is but one hope, "Return . . . amend your ways and your doings" (verse 11; cf. 7:3). But this is a hope which is no hope. The situation has gone too far. The call to turn is "in vain", useless (verse 12). The people are determined to pursue their own evil plans to the bitter end (see comment on 4:22).

STRANGELY UNNATURAL CONDUCT

Jeremiah 18:13–17

> [13]"Therefore thus says the Lord:
> Ask among the nations,
>   who has heard the like of this?
> The virgin Israel

has done a very horrible thing.
¹⁴Does the snow of Lebanon leave
    the crags of Sirion?
Do the mountain waters run dry,
    the cold flowing streams?
¹⁵But my people have forgotten me,
    they burn incense to false gods;
they have stumbled in their ways,
    in the ancient roads,
and have gone into bypaths,
    not the highway,
¹⁶making their land a horror,
    a thing to be hissed at for ever.
Every one who passes by it is horrified
    and shakes his head.
¹⁷Like the east wind I will scatter them
    before the enemy.
I will show them my back, not my face,
    in the day of their calamity."

The last passage ended by noting the determination of the people to persist in their evil ways. But Jeremiah is convinced that it ought not to be so. For Israel there is something unnatural in such conduct. He begins this passage by asking the same kind of surprised question that we heard in 2:11 (see comment). Israel has done something "horrible" or utterly shocking (verse 13). The fact that Israel is described here as "virgin Israel" (cf. 14:17), and the reference to burning incense to "false gods" (literally "something worthless") in verse 15, make it clear that this unnatural conduct consists of the way in which the people have prostituted themselves in the rituals associated with the worship of the fertility deities in Canaan. As the footnote to verse 14 in the RSV indicates, the text of this verse is very uncertain. Perhaps we get the flavour of what is being said, if we paraphrase and ask the following questions:

Does snow ever disappear off the summit of Mount Everest?
Does the source of the river Ganges ever dry up?

Nature is dependable, unchanging, but the people of Israel are fickle, irrational (cf. 8:7). They have stumbled in the ancient paths, the way God had mapped out for them in the covenant relationship (6:16); they have left the highway to turn, as it were, up a dirt track that leads to nowhere. How strange, how unnatural, and everyone seems to know it. Others regard Israel as something to be "hissed at" or whistled at (verse 16), an object of horrified amazement and revulsion. Everyone seems to know it, everyone except Israel. This perhaps is the only thing that is not strange in this situation, for are not we all often blind to the faults in ourselves that stick out a mile to other people?

> O wad some Pow'r the giftie gie us
> To see oursels as others see us!
> It wad frae mony a blunder free us,
>   And foolish notion.

> (Robert Burns, *To a Louse*)

But it is hard to see, far less to face, the truth about ourselves. It is the prophet's complaint that Israel seldom did, and because of that her fate is sealed. In from the desert will come the scorching east wind, to scatter them before the enemy, a reference to coming invasion by the Babylonians.

The passage ends with a homely illustration. When we are being friendly with someone, we look them in the face, we speak with them face to face. To express disapproval, or to indicate that we are offended, we turn our back. So the breakdown in the relationship between God and Israel, is indicated in the words of the Lord:

> I will show them my back, not my face,
>   in the day of their calamity.

OPPOSITION AND A VITRIOLIC RESPONSE

Jeremiah 18:18–23

[18]Then they said, "Come, let us make plots against Jeremiah, for the law shall not perish from the priest, nor counsel from the wise, nor the

word from the prophet. Come, let us smite him with the tongue, and let
us not heed any of his words."

¹⁹Give heed to me, O Lord,
    and hearken to my plea.
²⁰Is evil a recompense for good?
    Yet they have dug a pit for my life.
Remember how I stood before thee
    to speak good for them,
    to turn away thy wrath from them.
²¹Therefore deliver up their children to famine;
    give them over to the power of the sword,
let their wives become childless and widowed.
    May their men meet death by pestilence,
    their youths be slain by the sword in battle.
²²May a cry be heard from their houses,
    when thou bringest the marauder suddenly upon them!
For they have dug a pit to take me,
    and laid snares for my feet.
²³Yet, thou, O Lord, knowest
    all their plotting to slay me.
Forgive not their iniquity,
    nor blot out their sin from thy sight.
Let them be overthrown before thee;
    deal with them in the time of thine anger.

Jeremiah had been relentless in his criticism of the religious
leadership that was leading the nation to ruin (for priests, prophets, and wise men and their function in the community, see the
comments on 2:8, and 8:8–9). They reacted by taking steps to
discredit him and to silence him. It is the natural response of any
authoritarian system, be it political or religious, to the uncomfortable, dissenting voice. It takes many forms in our world today—
the labour camp, the psychiatric hospital, exile, manipulating the
media, withdrawing the right to teach, the dismissive comment
"Oh, he's a liberal . . . or an evangelical". "Come, let us smite
him with the tongue . . ." (verse 18) could mean generally to
revile him, to circulate slanderous gossip about him, or even to
bring formal legal charges against him. Whatever the technique,
its purpose was to justify their total indifference to the prophet's
message.

In response Jeremiah pleads with the Lord not to be indifferent to his plight: "Give heed to me, O Lord" (verse 19). Vehemently he protests that he has done nothing to deserve such treatment. On the contrary, he had tried to avert God's anger from the community by interceding in prayer for it (cf. 15:11). Then he rounds on his enemies in the most vitriolic cry for vengeance we hear on his lips (verses 21–23). Although there are parallels to such cries elsewhere in the Old Testament, notably in the Psalms of lament (e.g. Ps. 109:1–20) it is difficult not to be disturbed by Jeremiah's words, these "unevangelical prayers" as they have been called.

Some sensitive commentators have wished to delete these verses from the book as being unworthy of Jeremiah, but this is a desperate way out of a difficulty that we must try honestly to face. Attempts have been made to try to soften the impact of Jeremiah's harsh words by comparing them with Jesus' searing criticism of the scribes and the Pharisees in Matt. 23:13–39. But when the hatred of these same religious authorities took Jesus to a cross, the word from the cross is "Father, forgive them; for they know not what they do" (Luke 23:34), while Jeremiah can only bitterly say, "Forgive not their iniquity . . ." (verse 23). Nor does it help much to argue that Jeremiah is not reacting out of wounded pride to personal attacks; that he sees the opposition not merely as personal enemies but as God's enemies, that they are defying the word of the Lord and may therefore be rightly and roundly condemned without mercy. History is stained with the savage crimes of people who unquestioningly believed that they could justify what they were doing by claiming that it was the will of God.

Does this mean then that God's last word must therefore be "Forgive not . . ."? No, let us admit that here Jeremiah is flawed, not merely in the light of the cross, but even in the light of the deepest insights of the Old Testament. The servant of the Lord, in the book of Isaiah, accepts suffering, insult and opposition as part of his redemptive mission in the world. This was how God was bringing health and wholeness to others:

> He was oppressed, and he was afflicted,
> yet he opened not his mouth. (Isa. 53:7)

Jeremiah was oppressed and afflicted; but he opened his mouth and screamed down curses upon his oppressors. Flawed, yes, but for that very reason more truly one of us. The confessions show us no plaster-cast saint, but a man, warts and all; a man who often found faith difficult, who lived through periods of black despair, and who sometimes too easily identified his own raw emotions with the will of God. Flawed, yes, "Yet, thou, O Lord, knowest" (verse 23, cf. 12:3; 15:15). While these words in verse 23 enabled Jeremiah to draw strength from the fact that God shared his experience and was aware of the opposition which threatened the prophet's life, God also knew the kind of person Jeremiah was, took him just as he was, and still used him as his prophet over many long and troubled years. If God were not like that, there would not be much hope for any of us.

THE BROKEN JAR...

Jeremiah 19:1–13

¹Thus said the Lord, "Go, buy a potter's earthen flask, and take some of the elders of the people and some of the senior priests, ²and go out to the valley of the son of Hinnom at the entry of the Potsherd Gate, and proclaim there the words that I tell you. ³You shall say, 'Hear the word of the Lord, O kings of Judah and inhabitants of Jerusalem. Thus says the Lord of hosts, the God of Israel, Behold, I am bringing such evil upon this place that the ears of every one who hears of it will tingle. ⁴Because the people have forsaken me, and have profaned this place by burning incense in it to other gods whom neither they nor their fathers nor the kings of Judah have known; and because they have filled this place with the blood of innocents, ⁵and have built the high places of Baal to burn their sons in the fire as burnt offerings to Baal, which I did not command or decree, nor did it come into my mind; ⁶therefore, behold, days are coming, says the Lord, when this place shall no more be called Topheth, or the valley of the son of Hinnom, but the valley of Slaughter. ⁷And in this place I will make void the plans of Judah and Jerusalem, and will cause their people to fall by the

sword before their enemies, and by the hand of those who seek their life. I will give their dead bodies for food to the birds of the air and to the beasts of the earth. [8]And I will make this city a horror, a thing to be hissed at; every one who passes by it will be horrified and will hiss because of all its disasters. [9]And I will make them eat the flesh of their sons and their daughters, and every one shall eat the flesh of his neighbour in the siege and in the distress, with which their enemies and those who seek their life afflict them.'

[10]"Then you shall break the flask in the sight of the men who go with you, [11]and shall say to them, 'Thus says the Lord of hosts: So will I break this people and this city, as one breaks a potter's vessel, so that it can never be mended. Men shall bury in Topheth because there will be no place else to bury. [12]Thus will I do to this place, says the Lord, and to its inhabitants, making this city like Topheth. [13]The houses of Jerusalem and the houses of the kings of Judah—all the houses upon whose roofs incense has been burned to all the host of heaven, and drink offerings have been poured out to other gods—shall be defiled like the place of Topheth.'"

We have already followed Jeremiah into the potter's workshop (18:1–12). We have heard of Topheth and of the valley of Ben Hinnom, and their gruesome associations (see comment on 7:30–34). This narrative tells us about what Jeremiah did, in the valley of Ben Hinnom, with a finished product of the potter's skill, an "earthen flask" or "earthenware jar" (Hebrew *baqbuq*), a narrow-necked water decanter, of which many examples have come to light at excavated sites in Palestine. It reads like a straightforward story, but if you want to be a literary detective, there are clues scattered around which may lead you to conclude that we have here a mixture of more than one story or at least some pretty heavy-handed editorial work.

Read verses 1–2, then jump to verse 10. There is a simple story. Jeremiah is told to buy a decanter, take with him "some of the elders of the people and some of the senior priests" (verse 1), and then solemnly break the decanter "in the sight of the men who go with you" (verse 10). The point of this symbolic act is then drawn in the first half of verse 11, "Thus says the Lord of hosts: So will I break this people and this city, as one breaks a potter's vessel, so that it can never be mended". In verse 2 the phrase "the valley of the son of Hinnom at the entry of the Potsherd Gate" is rather odd. It would make sense if the incident happened simply "at the Potsherd Gate", whose location is unknown, but which is presumably so called because there the potters used to dump their spoiled and broken pieces of pottery.

Verses 3–9, however, contain a message addressed to "the kings of Judah and inhabitants of Jerusalem", the whole community from the highest to the lowest. It is a message of judgement, based on what has been going on at Topheth and in the valley of Ben Hinnom. This finds its natural continuation in the second half of verse 11. Much of the language in this section is closely related to what we find in the book of Deuteronomy, and it reads in fact like an expanded version of the earlier passage in 7:30–34.

Now literary detectives, like any other detectives, can get things wrong and follow false clues, but it is hard to escape the conclusion that the kernel of this incident is in verses 1–2, verse 10, and the first half of verse 11, in that jar which Jeremiah, at the Lord's command, smashed before a select group of influential citizens. In this symbolic act, the word is being presented as truly as in any words the prophet ever spoke. People and city are to be irrevocably broken. This message is neatly picked up in verse 7 where the verb translated in the RSV "I will make void" is similar in sound to the word for the jar or decanter, *baqbuq*. The NEB tries to catch the flavour of this by translating "I will shatter the plans of Judah and Jerusalem, as a jar is shattered". The prophet was certainly sounding a jarring note!

...AND ITS CONSEQUENCES

Jeremiah 19:14–20:6

[14]Then Jeremiah came from Topheth, where the Lord had sent him to prophesy, and he stood in the court of the Lord's house, and said to all the people: [15]"Thus says the Lord of hosts, the God of Israel, Behold, I am bringing upon this city and upon all its towns all the evil that I have pronounced against it, because they have stiffened their neck, refusing to hear my words."

¹Now Pashhur the priest, the son of Immer, who was chief officer in the house of the Lord, heard Jeremiah prophesying these things. ²Then Pashhur beat Jeremiah the prophet, and put him in the stocks that were in the upper Benjamin Gate of the house of the Lord. ³On the morrow, when Pashhur released Jeremiah from the stocks, Jeremiah said to him, "The Lord does not call your name Pashhur, but Terror on every side. ⁴For thus says the Lord: Behold, I will make you a terror to yourself and to all your friends. They shall fall by the sword of their enemies while you look on. And I will give all Judah into the hand of the king of Babylon; he shall carry them captive to Babylon, and shall slay them with the sword. ⁵Moreover, I will give all the wealth of the city, all its gains, all its prized belongings, and all the treasures of the kings of Judah into the hand of their enemies, who shall plunder them, and seize them, and carry them to Babylon. ⁶And you, Pashhur, and all who dwell in your house, shall go into captivity; to Babylon you shall go; and there you shall die, and there you shall be buried, you and all your friends, to whom you have prophesied falsely."

The word of judgement, dramatically portrayed in the shattered decanter, is then repeated for the benefit of all the people in "the court of the Lord's house" (verses 14–15). Presumably this took place before the time early in Jehoiakim's reign when Jeremiah was banned from preaching in the Temple precincts and began to record his preaching with the help of Baruch (see the Introduction and for the reference to banning 36:5). The result was predictable. The national shrine is not the place to preach what was tantamount to sedition and heresy. Steps were taken by the responsible Temple authorities to warn him off. A public flogging, a day "in the stocks" (20:2)—or in a prison cell (the Hebrew word could mean either)—would cool the hothead. Paul and Silas had a similar experience at the hands of the magistrates at Philippi (Acts 16:19–24).

The man responsible for law and order in the Temple precincts is "Pashhur the priest, the son of Immer" (20:1). Pashhur, which may be an Egyptian name, is not an uncommon name in the Old Testament; another Pashhur, the son of Malchiah, features in the narrative in 21:1 and 38:1. We can sympathise with Pashhur. He had a job to do, an important job, to ensure that things were done decently and in order in the Temple. People must not be needlessly disturbed or distracted when they come to worship God. Jeremiah could, no doubt, have broken decanters to his heart's content at the Potsherd Gate without Pashhur blinking an eyelid, but in the Temple precincts inflammatory words were not permitted.

This is not a case of personal animosity. We have here a clash of roles, similar to that which we find in the confrontation between the prophet Amos and the priest Amaziah at Bethel (Amos 7:10–17). Pashhur is there to safeguard the interests of the establishment; and every community needs a framework of law and order. Jeremiah, the voice of prophetic protest, is there not to make minor criticisms, but to pose a threat to the continuing existence of the establishment. There is probably no way in which either could understand the other's point of view, no more than the Ministry of Defence or the Pentagon can understand CND and the peace movement—and vice versa. Pashhur uses force in an attempt to silence Jeremiah. Jeremiah responds with a searing word of judgement, proclaiming in the Lord's name not only the destruction of the city at the hands of the Babylonians, but coming exile and death for Pashhur and his cronies. In the words, "The Lord does not call your name Pashhur, but Terror on every side" (20:3), there may be a play on the name Pashhur, though it is not wholly clear to us. For the phrase "Terror on every side" see the comments on 6:25 and 20:10. "Mr Law" is going to face the breakdown of law and order, and in the coming disorder his own fate is sealed.

INSIDIOUS DOUBT AND CONFIDENT FAITH

Jeremiah 20:7–13

7O Lord, thou hast deceived me,
    and I was deceived;
thou art stronger than I,
    and thou hast prevailed.
I have become a laughingstock all the day;
    every one mocks me

⁸For whenever I speak, I cry out,
   I shout, "Violence and destruction!"
For the word of the Lord has become for me
   a reproach and derision all day long.
⁹If I say, "I will not mention him,
   or speak any more in his name,"
there is in my heart as it were a burning fire
   shut up in my bones,
and I am weary with holding it in,
   and I cannot.
¹⁰For I hear many whispering.
   Terror is on every side!
"Denounce him! Let us denounce him!"
   say all my familiar friends,
   watching for my fall.
"Perhaps he will be deceived,
   then we can overcome him,
   and take our revenge on him."
¹¹But the Lord is with me as a dread warrior;
   therefore my persecutors will stumble,
   they will not overcome me.
They will be greatly shamed,
   for they will not succeed.
Their eternal dishonour
   will never be forgotten.
¹²O Lord of hosts, who triest the righteous,
   who seest the heart and the mind,
let me see thy vengeance upon them,
   for to thee have I committed my cause.

¹³Sing to the Lord;
   praise the Lord!
For he has delivered the life of the needy
   from the hand of evildoers.

The certainty that he had a word from the Lord, the courage to
proclaim it in face of opposition—that is the picture of Jeremiah
that emerges from the section 19:1–20:6. But there is the other
side to the story, the inner struggles, the uncertainties in the midst
of certainty, the confidence-sapping doubts that lurk beneath the
outward courage. To face Pashhur and rename him "Terror on

every side" is one thing, but what happens when that same nickname is mockingly hurled back at the prophet by people who have had more than they can stomach of this gloom and doom merchant (verse 10)?

No passage speaks more clearly of the spiritual tightrope on which Jeremiah was walking than this lament in 20:7–13, a lament which typically moves from crisis to confidence. The crisis is acute. Jeremiah begins with an embittered outburst, the full force of which hardly comes through in the RSV translation:

O Lord, thou hast deceived me, and I was deceived. (verse 7)

We are all given to harmless little deceptions at times, so why not God? But this is to trivialise what was for Jeremiah a harsh, soul-destroying experience. The word translated "deceived" and the following word rendered "thou art stronger than I" are both found elsewhere in the Old Testament in contexts which imply sexual seduction or rape (Exod. 22:16; Deut. 22:25). Jeremiah is protesting that he has been violated by a God whom he is not strong enough to resist. But what kind of violation is this? There may be an even sharper cutting edge to these words. The same word "deceived" is used in the story in 1 Kings chapter 22 where the Lord deliberately sends a lying spirit into Ahab's court prophets, and thus uses them to "deceive" Ahab and lure him to his doom. This then is the mission of the false prophet, to deceive, to seduce. Had the insidious thought lodged in Jeremiah's mind that perhaps the Lord was similarly playing with him, using him to deliver a false message?

It would not be a surprise if it had, since other people, including other prophets, had long been convinced that Jeremiah was wrong (see 17:14–18), a false prophet. Was he himself now seriously wrestling with that question? It is one of the marks of a mature spirituality that it is willing to face the question "suppose I am wrong?" Listen to the words of a radical Roman Catholic priest confronted with the teaching of the papal encyclical *Humanae Vitae* (1968) and with the threat of dismissal from his chaplaincy post because of his refusal to accept its teaching on contraception:

At first I was benumbed by the news, but numbness gave way to a mixture of feelings: pain, confusion, frustration and anger. How was I to act? In obedience to my conscience or to the papal encyclical? I had no problem in answering this question. The problem and the pain were in a further question. How do I know that my conscience is trustworthy, that I am not muddled in my thinking and blind through my own sinfulness? I had theoretical answers to all these questions, but they did not dispel the self-doubt (Gerald W. Hughes, *In Search of a Way*, p. 26).

Such self-doubt must have been there in Jeremiah, and it was so intense that, shaken by opposition and indifference, obsessed by the apparent failure of his ministry, he decided to call it a day:

I will not mention him [i.e. the Lord],
    or speak any more in his name. (verse 9*a*)

Only to discover that he could not! The choice was grim: to continue along the prophetic pathway facing "Terror on every side" and self-doubt, or to leave that pathway and stumble into a jungle of spiritual torment. To give up was not the way to peace. No longer to speak the word of the Lord! But then:

there is in my heart as it were a burning fire
    shut up in my bones,
and I am weary with holding it in,
    and I cannot. (verse 9*b*)

To go on was difficult, but not to go on was impossible. The God who had laid his hand upon him would not let him go. Not to believe, to refuse to live in the light of the vision we have received is seldom the easy option, however attractive it may sometimes seem.

But the God who would not let him go must surely, in spite of all doubts, be the God who would not let him down. There were ruthless, powerful enemies plotting his downfall (cf. 15:21; 20:1ff.), but the Lord was at his side "as a dread [or ruthless] warrior" (verse 11). The picture of the Lord as a warrior who does battle on behalf of his people is part of the liturgical tradition in which Jeremiah was nurtured. In the words of the great processional hymn, Psalm 24:

> Lift up your heads, O gates!
>> and be lifted up, O ancient doors!
>> that the King of glory may come in.
> Who is the King of glory?
>> The Lord, strong and mighty,
>> the Lord, mighty in battle! (Ps. 24:7–8)

So as this confidence surges back into him, Jeremiah bursts into a song of praise:

> Sing to the Lord;
>> praise the Lord!
> For he has delivered the life of the needy
>> from the hand of evildoers. (verse 13)

It may be that here Jeremiah is recalling a verse of a hymn with which he had long been familiar, though it occurs nowhere else in the Old Testament. Be that as it may, his song is a song of "the needy", the poor, the poor in spirit, those who are aware of their total dependence upon God (cf. Matt. 5:3).

There are some things that are more easily celebrated in song than in any other way. That is why the Easter hymns continue to be spiritually helpful and meaningful to many people who would be hard put to it to say in other ways what their thoughts about the resurrection were, or what they believe actually happened on that first Easter day. But if this song of Jeremiah's is a song of heavenly confidence, we have to remember that it is sung in the midst of a hell of despair.

THE DEPTHS OF DESPAIR

Jeremiah 20:14–18

> ¹⁴Cursed be the day
>> on which I was born!
> The day when my mother bore me,
>> let it not be blessed!
> ¹⁵Cursed be the man
>> who brought the news to my father,
> "A son is born to you,"

making him very glad.
¹⁶Let that man be like the cities
  which the Lord overthrew without pity;
let him hear a cry in the morning
  and an alarm at noon,
¹⁷because he did not kill me in the womb;
  so my mother would have been my grave,
  and her womb for ever great.
¹⁸Why did I come forth from the womb
  to see toil and sorrow,
  and spend my days in shame?

We have heard Jeremiah lamenting the fact that he was born to enter a world of ceaseless strife (15:10). This mood of despair and depression receives its most bitter expression in the curse that Jeremiah now calls down on the day of his birth. It hovers on the verge of blasphemy. Cursing one's parents, like cursing God, was a capital offence in ancient Israel (Lev. 20:9). Although Jeremiah does not curse his mother and his father, he curses "the day when my mother bore me" (verse 14); he curses the messenger who brought the glad news to his father "A son is born to you" (verse 15); and he wishes for that messenger a fate as violent and terrible as that which befell the corrupt cities of the plain, Sodom and Gomorrah (see Gen. 19:24–28). There is deep despondency in Jeremiah's words, the despondency of a man who feels he has reached the end of his tether, who sees the word "failure" written in large letters across his life. But if there is despondency, there is also an element of defiance, as if Jeremiah were shaking an angry fist at God as he screams "Why?" Why must life be like this "... toil and sorrow ... shame" (verse 18). To this "Why" there is no answer.

That this passage immediately follows the lament in verses 7–13 with its climax in the song of praise, should make us ponder anew what we have seen to be a recurring feature in these extracts from a prophet's spiritual diary. He was involved—for how long we know not—in a struggle for faith. There were days when the bottom seemed to have fallen out of his life, when his prophetic ministry looked like a meaningless charade. He could not stop the doubts coming; he had to live with them. He distrusted God; he had to learn painfully to distrust himself and his own swiftly changing emotions. The darkness threatened to overwhelm him; but in the darkness there was light, a flickering light, but it was one that the darkness was never able totally to extinguish.

In a concentration camp towards the end of the Second World War there died Dietrich Bonhoeffer, leader of the German Confessing Church, a pastor and theologian, who had written about and who knew well the cost of discipleship. From out of the hell of that concentration camp came his *Letters and Papers from Prison*. Much that is there in Jeremiah's confessions finds its echo in Bonhoeffer's experience. There is a prayer of Bonhoeffer's to which Jeremiah would surely have said a heartfelt "Amen".

In me there is darkness,
But with Thee there is light.
I am lonely, but Thou leavest me not.
I am restless, but with Thee there is peace.
In me there is bitterness, but with Thee there is patience;
Thy ways are past understanding,
   but Thou knowest the way for me.

(Letters and Papers from Prison, p. 32)

And there for the time being we must leave Jeremiah, holding on to faith amid the blackest despair—but the important thing is, holding on.

FURTHER READING

The books marked with an asterisk are suitable as an introduction to the study of Jeremiah

S. H. Blank, *Jeremiah: Man and Prophet* (Cincinnati 1961)

J. Bright, *Jeremiah* (Anchor Bible Vol. 21, New York 1965)

R. P. Carroll, *From Chaos to Covenant: Uses of Prophecy in the Book of Jeremiah* (London 1981)

* W. L. Holladay, *Jeremiah, Spokesman Out of Time* (Philadelphia 1974)

* E. W. Nicholson, *Jeremiah 1–25* (The Cambridge Bible Commentary on the NEB, Cambridge 1973)

J. Skinner, *Prophecy and Religion. Studies in the Life of Jeremiah* (Cambridge 1922)

J. A. Thompson, *The Book of Jeremiah* (Grand Rapids 1980)

- A. C. Welch, *Jeremiah, His Time and His Work* (Oxford 1951)